AF251800

THE SEVERITY OF GOD

This book explores the role of divine severity in the character and wisdom of God, and the flux and difficulties of human life in relation to divine salvation. Much has been written on problems of evil, but the matter of divine severity has received relatively little attention. Paul K. Moser discusses the function of philosophy, evidence, and miracles in approaching God. He argues that if God aims to extend without coercion His lasting life to humans, then commitment to that goal could manifest itself in making human life severe, for the sake of encouraging humans to enter into that cooperative good life. In this scenario, divine *agapē* is conferred as a free gift, but the human reception of it includes stress and struggle in the face of conflicting powers and priorities. Moser's work will be of great interest to students of the philosophy of religion and of theology.

PAUL K. MOSER is Professor of Philosophy at Loyola University Chicago. His most recent books include *The Elusive God: Reorienting Religious Epistemology* (Cambridge, 2009) and *The Evidence for God: Religious Knowledge Reexamined* (Cambridge, 2010). He is the editor of *Jesus and Philosophy: New Essays* (Cambridge, 2009) and co-editor, with Daniel Howard-Snyder, of *Divine Hiddenness* (Cambridge, 2002) and, with Michael McFall, of *The Wisdom of the Christian Faith* (Cambridge, 2012). Moser is the Editor of the *American Philosophical Quarterly*.

THE SEVERITY OF GOD

Religion and Philosophy Reconceived

PAUL K. MOSER

CAMBRIDGE
UNIVERSITY PRESS

CAMBRIDGE UNIVERSITY PRESS
Cambridge, New York, Melbourne, Madrid, Cape Town,
Singapore, São Paulo, Delhi, Mexico City

Cambridge University Press
The Edinburgh Building, Cambridge CB2 8RU, UK

Published in the United States of America by Cambridge University Press, New York

www.cambridge.org
Information on this title: www.cambridge.org/9781107023574

© Paul K. Moser 2013

This publication is in copyright. Subject to statutory exception
and to the provisions of relevant collective licensing agreements,
no reproduction of any part may take place without the written
. permission of Cambridge University Press.

First published 2013

Printed and bound in the United Kingdom by the MPG Books Group

A catalogue record for this publication is available from the British Library

Library of Congress Cataloguing in Publication data
Moser, Paul K., 1957–
The severity of God : religion and philosophy reconceived / Paul K. Moser.
pages   cm
Includes bibliographical references and index.
ISBN 978-1-107-02357-4 (hardback) – ISBN 978-1-107-61532-8 (paperback)
1. God (Christianity)   2. Worship.   3. Philosophy and
religion.   4. Philosophical theology.   I. Title.
BT103.M675 2013
212′.7–dc23
2012033990

ISBN 978-1-107-02357-4 Hardback
ISBN 978-1-107-61532-8 Paperback

Cambridge University Press has no responsibility for the persistence or
accuracy of URLs for external or third-party internet websites referred to in
this publication, and does not guarantee that any content on such websites is,
or will remain, accurate or appropriate.

For my mother, without whom not

Behold therefore the kindness and the severity of God
(Rom. 11:22)

Contents

Preface and acknowledgements

Human talk of God is often cheap and easy, and self-serving too. It thus leaves us with a god unworthy of the morally perfect title "God." This book takes a different route, in order to move away from counterfeits and toward the real article. Our expectations for God, if God exists, often get in the way of our receiving salient evidence of God. We assume that God would have certain obligations to us, even by way of giving us clear evidence, and when those obligations are not met we discredit God, including God's existence. This is a fast track to atheism or at least agnosticism. We need, however, to take stock of which expectations for God are fitting and which are not, given what would be God's perfect moral character and will.

Perhaps God is not casual but actually severe, in a sense to be clarified, owing to God's vigorous concern for the realization of divine righteous love (*agapē*), including its free, unearned reception and dissemination among humans. Perhaps the latter concern stems from God's aim to extend, without coercion, lasting life with God to humans, even humans who have failed by the standard of divine *agapē*. God's vigorous commitment to that goal could figure in God's making human life difficult, or severe, for the sake of encouraging humans, without coercion, to enter into a cooperative good life with God. This severe God would not sacrifice a human soul to preserve human bodily comfort. In this scenario, divine *agapē* is the unsurpassed power and priority of life with God, and humans need to struggle to appropriate it as such, in companionship with God. It comes as a free gift, by grace, from God, but the human reception of it, via cooperative trust in God, includes stress, struggle, and severity in the face of conflicting powers and alternative priorities.

This book attends to the widely neglected topic of the severity of God, in connection with its implications for religion and philosophy. It contends that divine severity points us to the volitional crisis of Gethsemane, for the sake of cooperative and lasting human life with God. In doing so, it invites us to consider the priority of divine power over philosophical propositions, persons over explanations, and God's will over human wills. Accordingly, this book invites us to reconceive religion and philosophy in the light of the Gethsemane crisis, particularly in the significant areas of the methodology and epistemology of God, the value of human life's ongoing flux, the divine redemption of humans, and the nature of philosophy under the severe God worthy of worship. This reconceiving leaves us with religion and philosophy renewed by a needed interpersonal and existential vitality, grounded in widely neglected but nonetheless salient evidence of God's redemptive severity.

My work has benefited from many people, too many to list here. For comments of various sorts, written or oral, I thank Tom Carson, Andrew Cutrofello, Robby Duncan, Blake Dutton, Stephen Joel Garver, Doug Geivett, Michael Haney, Chet Jechura, Myles Krueger, Jonathan Kvanvig, Michael McFall, Esther Meek, Chad Meister, Linda Moser, Harold Netland, Randy Newman, Gary Osmundsen, Alvin Plantinga, Bradley Seeman, Charles Taliaferro, David Yandell, Kate Waidler, Greg Wolcott, Tedla Woldeyohannes, Tom Wren, my philosophy students at Loyola University Chicago, and anonymous referees for Cambridge University Press. I also thank Robby Duncan for excellent help with the index.

Ancestors of parts of the book have appeared as, or were presented at: "*Agapēic* Theism: Personifying Evidence and Moral

Struggle," *European Journal for Philosophy of Religion*, 2 (2) (2010), pp. 1–18; "Religious Epistemology Personified: God without Natural Theology," in James Stump and Alan Padgett, eds., *The Blackwell Companion to Science and Christianity* (Blackwell, 2012), pp. 151–161; "God, Flux, and the *Agapē* Struggle," *Oxford Studies in Philosophy of Religion*, 4 (2012): 126–143; "Soteriology," in Chad Meister and James Beilby, eds., *The Routledge Companion to Modern Christian Thought* (Routledge, 2012); "Christianity and Miracles," in Chad Meister, J. P. Moreland, and K. Sweis (eds.), *Debating Christian Theism* (Oxford University Press, 2013); "Gethsemane Epistemology: Volitional and Evidential," *Philosophia Christi*, 14 (2) (2012); "Undermining the Case for Evidential Atheism," *Religious Studies*, 48 (1) (2012): 83–93; the Byron Bitar Memorial Lectures on divine severity at the Geneva College Philosophy Department (2011); the Harvard University Christian Union (2011); the APA Philosophy of Religion Group Symposium (2012; on my book, *The Evidence for God*); the Biola University Center for Christian Thought (2012); and the North Park University Philosophy Department (2012). I thank the original publishers for permission to draw from these ancestors, and I thank the various audiences for their helpful comments.

At Cambridge University Press, I thank Commissioning Editor Laura Morris, Assistant Editor Anna Lowe, Production Editor Christina Sarigiannidou, and their colleagues for excellent help in the editorial process. I also thank Emma Wildsmith and Liz Hudson for their fine work on the production and the copy-editing of the manuscript.

Introduction

> Christianity can falsely be made so severe that human nature must revolt against it … But Christianity can also be made so lenient or flavored with sweetness that all the attempts to perk up the appetite and give people a taste for it with demonstrations and reasons are futile and end up making people disgusted with it.
>
> (Kierkegaard 1851a, p. 203)

> Certainly no presentation of the Christian message today is likely to be of the least avail which does not hold firmly together both the goodness and the severity of God.
>
> (Farmer 1939, p. 112)

Christianity and theology aside, human life is severe in many ways, and, adding injury to insult, human death is no easier. Candor requires that we acknowledge as much, even though we humans seem to be unable to improve our predicament in any lasting way. If some children are sheltered from life's severity for a time, reality eventually intrudes, painfully and undeniably. This intrusion prompts humans to undertake all kinds of conduct for the sake of self-defense or at least temporary relief. Psychologists talk of human "coping mechanisms" and "diversionary tactics" in this connection.

Many people fold in the face of life's severity and settle for a kind of despair or hopelessness about human life. Bertrand Russell, for instance, recommended that a human life should be based "only on the firm foundation of unyielding despair" (1903, pp. 45–46). (It is doubtful that Russell was able to follow his own recommendation, given his aim to "instill faith in hours of despair," but that is a separate matter.) This book contends that life's severity does not underwrite a life of unyielding despair.

If *successful* coping requires neutralizing a problem, we evidently have unsuccessful coping in our *self*-management of life's severity. The severity persists despite the best human counter-efforts, and it resists being moderated in many cases. Self-medicating with nonprescription drugs, for instance, does not always neutralize our stress, even if it gets us through a night or two. In addition, if our source of self-medicating is addictive or otherwise destructive, we may end up worse off than when we began. At any rate, we should ask what, if anything, is the best response to the severity of human life. The answer depends, of course, on the nature of this severity.

SEVERITY

Severity can consist of a kind of stress or rigor that is free of evil but is nonetheless rigorously difficult for humans. For instance, not all stress in physical hunger or rigor in bodily exercise is evil in a morally relevant sense, but such stress can be severe indeed, owing to its rigorous difficulty for humans. It should go without saying that some evil is severe, even if severity does not entail evil. Despite voluminous discussion of logical and epistemological problems of evil, philosophers and theologians have given scarce attention to the problem of the severity of human life. In fact, no philosopher has offered a book-length work on severity regarding humans and God.

This book corrects for that deficiency in a manner that illuminates some important problems in the philosophy of religion. It attends to severity on both sides of the God–human relationship: severity as caused or at least allowed by God, and severity as experienced by humans.

The *Oxford English Dictionary* (2nd edn., 1989) offers this main definition of "severity": "strictness or sternness in dealing with others; stern or rigorous disposition or behaviour; rigour in treatment, discipline, punishment, or the like." This definition does *not* entail moral badness or evil, or any moral deficiency for that matter, contrary to some less prominent uses of "severity." The severity in question, however, does involve rigorous difficulty, discomfort, anxiety, stress, or insecurity for humans.

This book's problem, put broadly, is this: what sense, if any, can we make of the severity of human life? The desired "sense" would illuminate not only the nature of life's severity but also its value and its purposes, if it actually has value and purposes. This book contends that it does have underlying value and purposes and that this fact has significant implications for religion and philosophy and, more concretely, for the option of unyielding despair about human life. The relevant purposes, however, need not be transparent to all observers but can be "hidden" or "elusive," in a manner to be specified. What is true, for better or worse, need not be obviously true to everyone.

Some people will invoke God as an ultimate source to explain or otherwise to resolve at least some of life's severity. Other people will counter that an appeal to God in this connection is at best presumptuous and at worst misleading. Even so, this appeal may have some hope if inquirers have outside help, particularly divine help, as a source of information and other aid. This is a big "if," of course, but we cannot plausibly rule out this option at the start of inquiry, whatever we do with it later. This book gives this option a fair hearing, without any dogmatic favor or disfavor. In connection with (a notion of) God, the problem of divine severity becomes the problem of whether – and if so, why – a God worthy of worship would allow human life to be as severe or rigorously difficult as it actually is, at least at times. One might expect a God who vigorously cares for humans to blunt some of the severity faced by them and even more of the severity than is actually blunted in human life.

The book tries to make headway on the problem of severity by examining the distinctive character and purposes of a God worthy of worship. If this God seeks what is morally best for all people concerned, and not just a select few, then God may have definite redemptive purposes for human severity of various kinds. These purposes could go beyond supplying information to God's seeking profound transformation for humans, for the sake of human participation in God's perfect moral character. If this participation is part of what is morally best for humans, God could seek it even if severity, including divine severity, intrudes in human life. Severity would be part of the healing medicine prescribed for a human life in need of divine companionship and transformation toward God's moral character and will. We shall examine this proposal from several illuminating angles.

Many people, including philosophers, have misguided expectations for God. These expectations are misguided in their failing to match what would be God's relevant purposes, if God exists. The latter purposes include what God aims to achieve in revealing to humans (the evidence of) God's reality and will. Misguided expectations for God can leave one looking for evidence for God in all the wrong places. In failing to find the expected evidence, one easily lapses into despair, anger, or indifference toward matters of God. We find such regrettable attitudes among many people, including philosophers and theologians.

The needed antidote calls for a careful reconsideration of our expectations for God. This antidote enables us to approach religious epistemology in a way that does justice to the idea of a God worthy of worship. As we shall see, the evidence available to humans from a God worthy of worship would not be for mere spectators, but instead would seek to challenge the will of humans to cooperate with God's perfect will. This would result from God's seeking what is morally best for humans, including (a) their cooperative reconciliation to God, (b) their redemption from volitional corruption, such as selfishness, pride, and despair about human life, and (c) their ongoing cooperative life with God.

What if, as Kierkegaard (1846) suggested, God maintains God's value by refusing to become a mere third party and instead offering second-person (I–Thou) access to humans? What if, in addition, God is elusive in hiding from people unwilling to cooperate with God's will? Such "what if" questions can shake up misguided expectations for God and point us in a new, reliable direction. This book identifies that direction by acknowledging (a) the role of divine severity in the intended redemption of humans and, in our response, (b) the importance of human volitional cooperation with God, even when rigorous and unsettling.

PLANS

Characterized broadly, this book explores the role of divine severity in the following important areas: (a) the character and wisdom of God (Chapter 1); (b) the flux and struggle in human life (Chapter 2);

(c) the place of evidence, miracles, and arguments in human access to God (Chapter 3); (d) the divine salvation of humans (Chapter 4); and (e) the function of philosophy in approaching God (Chapter 5). These areas offer us an opportunity to clarify the character and purposes of divine severity via some outstanding problems in religion and philosophy. In fact, we shall see that divine severity prompts us to reconceive religion and philosophy in connection with these areas.

The book's unifying theme is that the kind of divine severity found in the volitional crisis of Gethsemane calls for reconceiving various problem areas in religion and philosophy. The reconceiving includes an intentional refocus from merely intellectual matters to existentially profound volitional matters in human priority relations to a severe God worthy of worship. Questions about human wills relative to God emerge as crucial in this reorientation. Religion and philosophy will look very different from this new perspective.

Chapter 1, "Severity and God," identifies how the moral character and will of a God worthy of worship would involve divine severity. In particular, it acknowledges that worthiness of worship requires moral perfection and that divine moral perfection demands that God seek to be redemptive toward all human candidates for redemption. It would not be adequate for God merely to want the redemption of humans. For the sake of moral perfection, God would have to do God's best to bring about human redemption for all genuine candidates. Because this would be the redemption of human *agents*, with their own wills, God would not be coercive in a manner that extinguishes or deactivates human wills. As a result, God's use of severity in human life to prompt redemption might not be a complete success story. Humans can resist, even stubbornly resist, redemption on God's terms, and some apparently do. Nothing necessitates that humans cooperate with God. Chapter 1 outlines how divine wisdom and severity figure in this predicament, and it portrays how human expectations of God can obscure the reality and purposes of God for humans. In addition, it offers a straightforward method to avoid the latter problem.

Chapter 2, "Severity and flux," asks how the flux, or impermanence, of this passing world bears on a case for a God worthy of worship. It contends that the bearing is positive rather than negative, given the redemptive character and aims of a God worthy of worship. It proposes that a severe *agapē* struggle involving humans and God is an elusive indicator of permanence in connection with this God. Philosophers of religion have neglected this important lesson, often as a result of looking for permanence in the wrong places. Chapter 2 identifies the upshot of this lesson for available human evidence of God. It offers a rather broad vision of such evidence that conforms to some important expectation-evoking questions regarding God's existence. Such a vision opens up some new prospects in the philosophy of religion by clarifying some key purposes behind divine severity, including the divine purpose of the volitional transformation of humans.

Chapter 3, "Severity and evidence," contends that a God worthy of worship would care about how a human fills in the following blank: "I inquire or believe regarding God's existence because I want ———." The chapter begins by asking what human motives we should expect God to want in human inquiry and belief regarding God. Resting on an expectation-evoking question regarding God's existence, this approach is widely neglected among philosophers, theologians, and others, but it can illuminate some important issues concerning divine severity and religious epistemology. Chapter 3 explains how this approach identifies the key shortcomings of the arguments of traditional natural theology. It indicates that such arguments fail to accommodate the motives that God, as worthy of worship, would want in human inquiry and belief regarding God. Chapter 3 also contends that we should not expect a God worthy of worship to supply observable miracles to humans on demand, because divine redemption would aim for the profound moral transformation of humans independent of such miracles. In other words, the severity of divine grace in human redemption has no absolute need for such miracles among humans. The chapter contends that we should formulate our expectations of God accordingly.

Chapter 4, "Severity and salvation," argues that a defensible approach to salvation by divine "grace," including divine redemptive severity, requires an active, cooperative role for humans in their salvation. Identifying this active role, the chapter elucidates the indispensability of human accountability and cooperation in the realization of human salvation, and it suggests that this contributes to an understanding of divine severity in human salvation. Chapter 4 clarifies this active role via a distinction between (a) an action that either *constitutes* or *earns* salvation and (b) an action that *receives* already constituted salvation. The chapter illuminates the nature of divinely reckoned righteousness to humans via human faith that is active in the salvation involving the human reception of divine power. It contends that the severity of worthiness of worship calls for such distinctive righteousness among humans but blocks any role for human self-righteousness or humanly earned salvation.

Chapter 5, "Severity and philosophy," assumes that divine severity is a morally loaded sifting project in human redemption by a God worthy of worship who refuses to extinguish human agency. This severity involves divine sifting with regard to human receptivity toward divine grace anchored in a gift of righteousness as cooperative life with God for amenable humans. As personified in Jesus Christ, this grace seeks to inhabit human lives as their forgiving Lord and transformative Sustainer. Chapter 5 contends that this inhabiting comes via a rigorous kind of human receptivity, specifically via a union in divine *agapē* whereby one dies and rises with Christ into a self-sacrificial life with a severe God worthy of worship. It finds, accordingly, the distinctive focus of Christian philosophy in the redemptive *power* of God in Christ, available in the severity of human experience and life. This power transcends philosophical wisdom by delivering the causally powerful Spirit of God, who intervenes with a goal of divine corrective reciprocity. The chapter indicates that this power yields a distinctive religious epistemology and even a special role for Christian spirituality in Christian philosophy. It also challenges an influential counter from philosophical atheism.

Overall, the book's lesson is that only a severe God would be worthy of worship, but such a God would be severely redemptive and thus vigorously transformative in a manner that overturns business as usual in religion, theology, philosophy, and related disciplines. The remaining question is whether humans are truly receptive to this divine solution to their rigorous predicament. Answers will vary among humans, of course, but this book contends that we should acknowledge the crucial human responsibility in this area of inquiry. We shall see, in the end, how human inquirers are themselves under vigorous divine inquiry in this vital area, whatever their actual expectations of God. Inquirers of God, then, become themselves a focus of morally relevant divine inquiry and therefore have no exemption from accountability before the severe God who is worthy of worship. We shall see how religion and philosophy look from this new perspective.

Severity and God

The Lord your God is a devouring fire, a jealous God.
(Deut. 4:24, NRSV; cf. Heb. 12:29)

When we have seen God as Christ saw Him, as One who is
infinitely austere in His demands on *Himself* for our sakes, One
in whose heart is the final self-surrender which we see in the
Cross, then to give all, if necessary, for Him will not merely
seem a reasonable demand ... but a joy and an opportunity
which we would not miss.
(Farmer 1939, p. 54)

Talk of "divine severity" calls, of course, for a conception of the
divine, or of God. It also would be helpful to have some sense of
God's purposes, if God exists, in relating to humans and the severity
in their lives. This chapter offers some illumination on these fronts,
in order to suggest how divine severity can fit with the perfect goodness of a God worthy of worship.

GOD AND GRACE

Worthiness of worship

Setting the bar high, indeed as high as possible, we will approach
the term "God" as a supreme title of personal perfection rather
than a proper name. (We can always lower the bar if our overall

evidence calls for this.) Likewise, some variants of monotheism suggest that the term "God" is a normative title requiring *worthiness of worship*. Given such a title, no mere potentate who dominates over all others will qualify as God. Something beyond domination is needed, because *worthiness* of worship is needed. Such worthiness is normative, not merely descriptive, and therefore does not support the false claim that "might makes right." According to this view, "God" is not God's name, because the term "God" is a normative title. A title can be meaningful but lack a titleholder. In talking about God, then, we can give a fair hearing to proponents of atheism and agnosticism without begging questions against them or otherwise dismissing them.

Characteristically, worship involves not only adoration and submission but also a welcoming commitment to the perfect goodness and authority of the recipient of worship. Worthiness of worship, as many people understand it, requires of a recipient of worship the worthiness of a person's commitment to, or trust in, the perfect goodness and authority of that recipient. A morally defective recipient will not merit one's commitment to, or trust in, its perfect goodness and authority, because its moral defectiveness will undermine such goodness and authority in the area of morality. Accordingly, a morally defective recipient will not be worthy of worship, even if some people actually (and mistakenly) worship this recipient. A candidate for being God, then, must *merit* unqualified trust in the perfect goodness and authority of that candidate.

Something will be worthy of worship only if it is morally without defect, that is, morally perfect. Something (or, better, someone) will satisfy the title "God," then, only if that thing (or one) is morally perfect, and this perfection must be inherent rather than borrowed. If humans could borrow moral perfection from God they still would fail to be worthy of worship. As a result, inquirers about God should attend to the character of a morally perfect agent whose perfection is inherent. Failure to do so would amount to failure to consider God as worthy of worship, and the latter failure is common among inquirers about the existence of God, particularly when their focus is on God as a first cause or a designer of the universe.

The normative title "God" offers a moral criterion to adjudicate candidates, however powerful they are. As suggested, God must merit being God on moral grounds. No big bad bully, therefore, will qualify as being God just in virtue of strength, power, or even omnipotence. An impeccable moral standing is needed, and this excludes all of the candidates who, however powerful, do evil to get their way. Being God does not allow for getting your way however you wish, because moral perfection must be preserved.

Even if we disagree about some of the details of moral goodness, moral perfection requires one's seeking what is morally best for all concerned. God, then, would have to go beyond mere kindness or even mercy to seek what is morally best for all concerned, not just for God's allies. This goal would be a divine purpose without which one would not be divine. God, then, is not to be confused with the kind of evil being called "Satan." As for humans, they might or might not have the exalted goal of seeking what is morally best for all concerned.

In seeking what is morally best for all concerned, God would be morally caring toward all other persons, even toward enemies of God. This would raise the moral bar high for candidates for God. They could not hate their enemies by seeking their personal destruction; instead, they would have to seek the moral well-being of their enemies as well as their allies (although intended recipients could freely resist). This would take us beyond familiar human standards for handling enemies to a divine standard of universal moral care. This standard may seem foolish, given our selfish and prideful ways, but it is required by the moral perfection in worthiness of worship and being God. God, accordingly, could not be passive but would have to be active toward all others for the sake of their moral well-being. So, Aristotle's god in Book Lambda of his *Metaphysics*, characterized in terms of "thought thinking itself," is not the true God worthy of worship; likewise for many other candidates, past and present. These candidates fall short of the high moral standard for God.

God's activity would be *purposive*, that is, guided by a purpose or goal regarding others. This purpose involves a divine aim to give *morally impeccable life* to others noncoercively and lastingly, in their companionship, reverence, and worship of God. The giving of such life would include God's delivering people from what obstructs a morally good life, and God's empowering the killing of anti-God behavior, without extinguishing human wills. If God extinguished human wills, humans themselves would be extinguished as candidates for genuine moral relationships and companionship with God, thus undermining God's redemptive purpose. The grand purpose in question is God's aim to give *deep, volitional deliverance* to humans. Such deliverance is volitionally deep in its serious moral and spiritual concern, and it includes a cooperative rescue from human moral and spiritual shortcomings that block a cooperative life with God. It frees humans from their selfishness and lack of forgiveness for the sake of a life in reverent companionship with God and in *agapē* and forgiveness toward others, even enemies.

By analogy, consider a lifeguard at a Lake Michigan beach. In rescuing a drowning person, the lifeguard draws from personal power beyond the drowning person, but the drowning person (if conscious) needs to cooperate with the rescuer. So, the source of the rescuing power does not belong to the drowning person, but the drowning person still must exercise his power of cooperation with the lifeguard. Likewise, if God has the power to rescue humans in moral trouble, they still may need to cooperate with the rescuing power on offer. Humans may need to cooperate with a rescue *on God's morally perfect terms*, instead of assuming that they can set the terms of their rescue. This lesson should be no surprise if God is morally perfect and we humans are not. Even so, many humans presume that they can set the terms for God's rescue of humans and for suitable evidence of God's reality, but this false presumption obscures the evidence and the reality of God for them. It obstructs human apprehension of God, given what would be God's purposes in deliverance and in self-manifestation.

God's deep deliverance of humans would differ from an ordinary lifeguard rescue. It would require the moral transformation of a human and not just the extension of a human life. So, an ordinary lifeguard cannot fill in for God; a more powerful rescuer is needed, because humans as moral agents need something beyond the mere extension of their lives. Perhaps humans are drowning in something or other, but, in any case, more than the length of their lives is at risk. We might think of the *moral quality* of our personal characters as a big part of our problem, at least from the perspective of a morally perfect God. What, then, would such a God do with humans like us? This question is important, but it rarely gets careful attention from philosophers.

Perhaps inquirers about God are typically, if unknowingly, too *world-bound* in their thinking and living to give a fair hearing to the evidence and the reality of God. By "world-bound," I mean one's being directed away from God's morally perfect character to worldly attitudes and behaviors, including selfish, prideful, or despairing decisions, which conflict with God. One result would be human distortion, if unknowing, in the assessment of the evidence and the reality of God. This would include a human tendency to look for the evidence of God in places that may meet *human* expectations of God, such as worldly power and success, but conflict with God's actual moral character. Let's develop this idea a bit.

Human religion and the human assessment of religion are often not *deeply experiential and volitional* in the way suited to God's morally perfect character. Being deeply experiential and volitional in the right way would open one to direct confrontation, including in one's conscience, with a convicting God who seeks to give deep deliverance. For the sake of redeeming humans, this God would bring serious *conflict* to deep human experience and volition: that is, a conflict between God's morally perfect will and the various human ways at odds with that will. God, then, would not be one who gives humans *mere* affirmation, tranquility, or amazement, or even mere kindness or mercy. Much contemporary discussion of God's existence suffers from consideration of an inferior counterfeit and thus misses the high mark regarding a God worthy of worship.

When the dust of historical inquiry settles, plausible candidates for the title "God" (in terms of worthiness of worship) are few and far between. In fact, many people doubt that there is even one serious candidate, given the requirement of moral perfection in the titleholder. The successful candidate must be not just good on balance or good typically but morally good *without exception*. Clearly, therefore, ordinary humans do not qualify for the title, even if some humans consider themselves good and are, in fact, good in various ways. Typically, the moral character of humans is defective to some extent, however commendable it is in some respects. Human selfishness abundantly illustrates this mundane but pertinent lesson.

Perfect moral goodness in an agent combines the impeccable moral goodness *within* the agent (or, in the agent's own internal character) and the similar goodness of the agent *toward* (or, in relation to) all other agents and situations. If we call such twofold goodness of an agent "righteousness," we can distinguish between an agent's *individual* righteousness and an agent's *relational* righteousness. Perfect moral goodness in an agent requires both perfect individual righteousness and perfect relational righteousness in that agent. Any morally inferior agent will fall short of perfect goodness, even if that agent is praiseworthy for a less exalted status. A typical human agent, for instance, qualifies as such a morally inferior agent and hence fails to merit the title "God."

Perfect relational righteousness includes not just general moral decency but also merciful and compassionate righteous love, or *agapē*, toward all agents, including one's enemies. Such *agapē* exceeds feelings or emotions in requiring a person (when the opportunity arises) to *will*, without coercion, what is morally best for all agents affected. A bearer of perfect relational righteousness would seek to manifest individual righteousness, such as in morally commendable actions, for the good of all involved. In addition, this bearer would seek to instill, without coercion, individual and relational righteousness in all agents affected.

Regarding a coercive will, John Oman observes, "the might which is irresistible, because it breaks what it cannot bend, is not the greatest" (1928, p. 245). This holds true if God aims to preserve genuine human agency in ethical decisions by humans. In that case, God would seek noncoercively to instill individual and relational righteousness in willing people, in order to bring perfect moral goodness to them. God, then, would not be static in righteousness by keeping it inactive and restricted to God. Instead, God would be active in righteousness by seeking to proliferate it within and among agents, without robbing them of their genuine agency in ethical decisions.

As indicated by our moral imperfections, humans lack the power of their own to meet a standard of perfect individual or relational righteousness. For instance, humans are in no position to claim that they have satisfied the commandment to love others, including their enemies, unselfishly. Human selfishness has intruded in a manner that violates this love commandment, and the consequences often have been harmful to the people affected. Accordingly, we may question psychological stability when a human emerges with a claim to possess perfect righteousness, including perfect love of enemies. At the least, we recognize that talk is cheap in such a case.

Divine grace

Given human failure in perfect righteousness, any divine redemption, or salvation, of humans aimed at such righteousness for humans must have a distinctive status. This is the status of an unearned, unmerited gift of "grace" (*charis*), to use a term from some letters in the New Testament. Divine grace stands in contrast not to human action or deed (contrary to many theorists) but rather to something earned or merited by humans. (Chapter 4 develops this theme.) The idea is that human moral standing before God does not obligate God to offer redemption, but God, out of graciousness, offers redemption anyway, to be appropriated undeservedly by humans. If God's grace comes to humans, then, it comes on *God's* perfect terms, and not on human terms of earning or merit. So, the idea of a free, unmerited gift of salvation would be appropriate, even if unexpected by humans. We need to clarify this widely misunderstood idea, because divine grace, although a redemptive gift, can be rigorous in its expectations of recipients and in its appropriation by recipients.

H. R. Mackintosh has contrasted classical Greek and New Testament understandings of grace:

Classical writers mean by *charis* that which gives pleasure or delight, and so loveliness or charm ... The profounder meaning of the word in primitive Christianity – viz., the unmerited Divine love which stoops to pardon and bless the guilty – is, in part, a heritage from the Old Testament, but it draws its characteristic intensity from the felt presence of redeeming love in Jesus Christ … By grace [the apostle Paul] means the free love of God, visiting [humans] even when unsought, more particularly as opposed to all demands of law or claims of merit. (1928, p. 365; cf. Mackintosh 1927, pp. 129–130)

According to some of the earliest Christians, grace concerns God's redemptive, or salvific, intervention on behalf of humans without their earning or meriting such intervention.

As suggested, God's intervention stems from a gracious character of divine *agapē* and brings an offer of pardon, or forgiveness, and even of divine companionship to humans. This offer comes as a generous gift from God, and not as something earned or deserved by humans. Even so, the offer could come with rigorous divine expectations for humans concerning their response, such as their taking the offer seriously and responding wholeheartedly and reverently. Accordingly, an expected response to an offer is not necessarily a response that earns or merits the offer.

Following Paul, Karl Barth has identified a role for the *power* of a personal agent in divine grace:

Grace is the generous and free will of God, His will to accept us … Grace is, then, no spiritual power residing in the [hu]man of this world; no physical energy residing in Nature; no cosmic power in this earth. Grace is and remains always the Power of God (Rom. 1:16), the promise of a new [hu-]man, of a new nature, of a new world: it is the promise of the Kingdom of God … Restless, and terribly shattering, grace completely overthrows the foundations of this world; and yet … the operation of grace [is] no mere negation. Grace is … salvation, comfort, and edification. (1933, p. 59)

In Paul's perspective, divine grace is the empowering gift of life from a divine personal agent for receptive humans, and this agent enters into judgment as corrective inquiry in human experience. (Chapter 3 returns to this kind of inquiry.) The gift is intended to empower humans to become renewed, reconciled members of

God's kingdom family, in life together with God and with each other. Humans, however, are not coerced by this grace; it does not rob them of their personal agency and responsibility before God. (For illuminating discussion in this regard, see Oman 1919.)

The source of grace in a divine promise favoring humans indicates both its being unearned by humans and its stemming from a gracious divine character. According to this perspective, God intervenes powerfully in human lives to offer salvation as life in cooperation with God, despite humans' not deserving this gift of reconciliation. Human habits of selfishness and pride resist this gift and therefore call for a rigorous, even severe, divine challenge to humans. This challenge, we shall see, is very different from the divine coercion of humans, because it leaves human agency intact. Even so, it brings severity of human life in its wake, and this phenomenon is widely misunderstood.

A bearer of perfect grace (and righteousness and *agapē*) could not be casual about manifesting and offering grace for others. Moral laxness here would entail a moral defect and hence moral imperfection. Accordingly, the divine vigor in manifesting and offering grace would have to be morally perfect, without moral defect. A gift of divine grace would have to be offered with moral perfection even in its intensity and rigor. It therefore would avoid doing any moral harm or damage to others, such as an immoral extinguishing of their moral agency. Grace that does moral harm fails automatically to be perfect grace and hence fails to be divine grace. Similarly, any divine judgment of others must be free of immorality for God to be worthy of worship.

A perfectly rigorous offer of divine grace may call for a divine *self*-offering to humans that offers shared life with God while preserving human agency. John Oman suggests this prospect: "What would make [people] at once righteous and free is not the force which would subdue to an ungracious submission, but the omniscient devices of [divine] self-sacrifice to win the consent of the [human] heart" (1928, p. 246). This prospect summarizes the central message in the New Testament, regarding the death and resurrection of Jesus Christ as God's self-giving representative for humans. The present book gives a fair hearing to this prospect, with special attention to divine severity in the redemption of humans.

The central New Testament message portrays divine grace as culminating in the self-sacrificial life, death, and resurrection of Jesus Christ, in keeping with God's will for human redemption. According to this message, the self-offering of Jesus to God on behalf of humans includes an invitation to humans to share God's life of perfect righteousness. The human response ideally includes self-giving trust in God (and in Jesus as God's representative), because God seeks to have humans relate to God freely, reverently, and wholeheartedly. The divine redemption of humans, according to this message, seeks to have humans share God's morally perfect life as God's reconciled, dependent children. In sharing God's life, humans are to become self-giving in the way God is (and Jesus is). From this perspective, human life is an ongoing challenge from God to enter into companionship with God, under divine authority. Humans can meet this challenge, however, only in cooperation with God, and not in their own power.

The status of humans as creatures dependent on God would indicate real limits, even discomforting limits, in human power relative to God. Such limits would recommend against humans' playing God or presuming a level of authority, understanding, or wisdom suited to God alone. The wisdom possessed by humans, accordingly, may be sharply limited and thus incomplete in some important areas, including in inquiry about God. Real limits persist for humans, despite faith in God. Even so, God's wisdom recommends severity in the divine redemption of humans, and therefore we should attend to this intriguing wisdom, even if our current understanding of it is limited.

DIVINE WISDOM PERSONIFIED

Western philosophy emerged with the concerns of Socrates and Plato about wisdom (*sophia*). Socrates launched a discussion of wisdom as follows:

> I shall call as witness to my wisdom, such as it is, the god at Delphi … I am only too conscious that I have no claim to wisdom, great or small. So what can he mean by asserting that I am the wisest man in the world? He cannot be telling a lie; that would not be right for him … The truth of the matter … is pretty certainly this, that real wisdom is the property of God, and this oracle is his way of telling us that human wisdom has little or no value. It seems to me that he is not referring literally to Socrates, but has merely taken my name as an example, as if he would say to us, The wisest of you men is he who realized, like Socrates, that in respect of wisdom he is really worthless. (*Apology*, 20e, 21b, 23a–b, trans. H. Tredennick; cf. *Phaedrus* 278d)

Wisdom, according to Socrates and Plato, leads to happiness (*Meno*, 88c) but requires a kind of human "purification" (*Phaedo*, 69c), because it provides an escape from evil (*Phaedo*, 107c–d). In the *Laws*, Plato portrays the Athenian as stating: "righteousness, temperance, and wisdom [are] our salvation, and these have their home in the living might of the gods, though some faint trace of them is also plainly to be seen dwelling here within ourselves" (10.906b, trans. A. E. Taylor).

In Plato's portrait, wisdom belongs to God (not humans), counters evil, and contributes to human happiness and even "salvation." Platonic salvation via wisdom includes the deliverance of the human mind / soul from the vicissitudes of change into acquaintance with the immutable and invisible constituents of reality (see *Phaedo*, 79). Plato's portrait of wisdom is widely rejected by contemporary philosophers, partly because most Western philosophers now aim to avoid reliance on God in their philosophy. Even so, Plato offered an approach to wisdom that merits comparison with a Christian approach. If "real wisdom is the property of God," as Plato claimed, then wisdom is theological. We shall ask whether Plato was on the right track and, if so, what role God and divine severity have in wisdom. A contrast with the apostle Paul will illuminate our inquiry.

Wisdom from Paul

The apostle Paul's approach to wisdom differs from Plato's, but Paul also acknowledges God as the source of human wisdom. Here we find a neglected analogy between Paul's view of wisdom and his understanding of righteousness, or justification (*dikaiosunē*). We can use his approach to righteousness to introduce his view of wisdom.

Paul regards the salvation of humans as their being *reconciled* to God, by means of a powerful manifestation of God's moral character in Jesus Christ. He states, "in Christ God was reconciling the world to himself, not counting their trespasses against them" (2 Cor. 5:19, NRSV, here and in subsequent biblical quotations, unless otherwise noted). According to Paul, Jesus is God's representative victim (of human opposition) who offers divine forgiveness as well as companionship, instead of condemnation, to humans. Let's call this *the divine manifest-offering* approach to salvation, in keeping with Romans 3:21–26 (which mentions divine manifestation repeatedly). What is being made *manifest* in Jesus Christ is God's moral character of righteous and forgiving love, and what is being *offered* in Jesus Christ, in keeping with God's character, is life-giving companionship with God as a divine gift under divine authority.

In Paul's story, the divine gift for humans is anchored in (a) the forgiveness offered and manifested via God's self-giving sacrifice in Jesus Christ, and (b) God's resurrection approval of Jesus as Lord and as Giver of God's Spirit. The manifestation of God's character in Jesus reveals a God who offers forgiveness and lasting companionship to humans for the sake of their salvation. The death of Jesus by itself does not bring about divine–human reconciliation, but it does aim to provide God's means of implementing salvation via divine manifestation and offering. For actual divine–human reconciliation, humans must *receive*, or *appropriate*, the manifest offering of forgiveness and companionship via grounded trust, or faith, in God. Such human cooperation with God figures crucially in the divine redemptive plan.

According to Paul, Jesus Christ as Lord and as Giver of God's Spirit came from God to identify with us humans in our weakness and despair, in order to offer us life with God (1 Thess. 5:9–10), while he represented God in righteous and merciful *agapē* (Rom. 5:6–8). As God's befriending mediator for humans, Jesus aims to represent, and to offer a personal bridge between, God *and* humans. Specifically, he seeks to reconcile humans to God with the gift of companionship anchored in merciful *agapē* as the power of God's Spirit. This Good News, according to Paul, is inherently theological and Christological and hence cannot be reduced to a story of morality or ethics.

Jesus Christ's death on the cross, commanded of him by God (Rom. 3:25; 1 Cor. 5:7; Phil. 2:8; cf. Mark 14:23–24), aims to manifest how far he and God will go to offer salvation to humans. By divine plan, Jesus gives humans all he has, from God's self-giving love, to manifest that God mercifully and righteously loves humans to the fullest. Jesus thereby offers humans salvation as the gift of unearned forgiveness, companionship, and membership in God's family via reception of God's Spirit (see Rom. 5:8; cf. John 3:16–17). This is the heart of the Good News of divine salvation for humans that Paul announced in the first century, to philosophers and others.

Paul proclaims the cross of Jesus Christ as the place where human rebellion against God is mercifully judged and forgiven by God. This does *not* mean that God punished Jesus, a reportedly innocent man before God. No New Testament writer teaches otherwise, contrary to some later, more speculative theologians. According to Paul, God sent Jesus into this world to undergo, willingly, suffering and death at human hands. God, in Paul's story, mercifully deems this intervention adequate for dealing justly with human rebellion against God. In this respect, Jesus paid the price on behalf of humans for the divine reconciliation of humans. In manifesting and offering divine forgiveness and companionship, he thereby offers an alternative to selfish fear, condemnation, shame, and guilt among humans toward God (see Rom. 8:1).

Paul identifies the key motive for the crucifixion of Jesus as (the manifestation of) God's *righteous love* for humans. Unlike many later theologians, Paul links God's righteousness, or justice, with God's *agapē*:

God manifests his own *agapē* for us in that while we were yet sinners, Christ died for us … Since we have now been justified by his blood, how much more shall we be saved by him from the wrath [of God] … [W]hile we were enemies [of God], we were reconciled to God through the death of his Son. (Rom. 5:8–10)

According to Paul, God takes the initiative and the means through Jesus Christ in offering a gift of divine–human reconciliation for salvation. As suggested, Paul finds the self-sacrificial death of Jesus to manifest forgiving *agapē* and righteousness, and he thinks of divine *agapē* as morally robust in being *righteous*. As we shall see, the importance of divine righteousness contributes to the role of severity in the divine redemption of humans.

In Paul's story, the mere forgiveness of humans by God would fail to counter the wrongdoing that called for forgiveness, namely, the human neglect of the divine authority needed for a lasting good life (see Rom. 1:21, 28). In exposing and judging the basis of human wrongdoing, God upholds moral integrity in the divine salvation of humans, without condoning evil. Through the self-sacrifice of Jesus, according to Paul, *God* meets the standard of perfect *agapē* for us humans, when we could not and would not. God then offers this gift of righteousness to us, as God's Passover lamb for us (1 Cor. 5:7), to be received by trust in God and Jesus. Otherwise, our prospect for meeting the standard of divine *agapē* (and thus for salvation by God's perfect standard) would be bleak indeed, and human despair would threaten and even prevail.

Paul focuses on *gift*-righteousness from God to receptive humans, in contrast to *earned* righteousness via, for instance, the Mosaic law (see Phil. 3:9, Rom. 3:21–26, 10:3–4, Gal. 3:11–12). Because humans have failed by the standard of divine *agapē*, they are in no position to *earn*, or *merit*, a right relationship with God. If such a relationship is to be realized, this must come from something other than human earning because such earning has failed. The needed alternative, according to Paul, is the divine *gift* of salvation by grace (*charis*) offered to undeserving humans. Humans still need to struggle to *appropriate* this gift, through the rigorous stresses of trust and obedience toward God, but this struggle does not involve our earning or meriting God's approval. Acts of obedience to God, accordingly, are not identical with works of earning or merit before God, despite frequent confusions in this area. (See Romans 4:4 for Paul's linking of "works" in the relevant sense with an earning, or a paying a debt, toward God; Chapter 4 returns to this matter in detail.)

We now can make sense of Paul's approach to wisdom as a rigorous gift from God. Paul draws from Isaiah 29:14 that God aims to "destroy the wisdom of the wise" (1 Cor. 1:19; cf. 3:18–20) in order to undermine human boasting in humans rather than in God (1 Cor. 1:29–31; cf. 3:21). Paul holds that for a lasting good life, as an alternative to despair (cf. 2 Cor. 4:8), humans need to rely on God's wisdom and power instead of a human alternative. Human reliance on God's wisdom and power, however, is no casual matter; it requires dying to human anti-God ways in order to live cooperatively with God. It thus requires one's struggling with oneself.

Paul states regarding himself: "My speech and my proclamation were not with plausible words of wisdom, but with a demonstration of the Spirit and of power, *so that* your faith might rest not on human wisdom but on the power of God" (1 Cor. 2:4–5; italics added). Paul then contrasts "human" wisdom with "God's wisdom, secret and hidden, which God decreed before the ages for our glory" (1 Cor. 2:7). The key difference between the two is that God's wisdom has the divine *power* (*dunamis*), including the power of self-giving *agapē*, to give a *lasting good life* to receptive humans, as an alternative to despair, whereas human wisdom does not. Only God's wisdom can empower human salvation as a lasting good life anchored in good, self-giving personal relationships under God.

We can see the role of human weakness, or impotence, in relation to God's power. Paul remarks: "we have this treasure [of salvation from God] in clay jars, *so that* it may be made clear that this extraordinary power belongs to God and does not belong to us" (2 Cor. 4:7; italics added; cf. Savage 1996). The power and wisdom needed by humans, according to Paul, must come from God, because God alone has such power and wisdom. In writing to Christians at Colossae, Paul describes the relevant power and wisdom:

We have not ceased praying for you and asking that you may be filled with the knowledge of God's will in all spiritual wisdom and understanding, so that you may lead lives worthy of the Lord, fully pleasing to him, as you bear fruit in every good work and as you grow in the knowledge of God. May you be made strong [= empowered] with all the strength [= power, *dunamis*] that comes from his glorious power, and may you be prepared to endure everything with patience, while joyfully giving thanks to the Father. (Col. 1:9–12)

Paul's "spiritual wisdom" is not mere knowledge that a claim is true; instead, it is directed toward "lead[ing] lives worthy of the Lord, fully pleasing to him." It welcomes God's power for the sake of joyfully enduring the severity of life with patience. This is the power to endure life while honoring and thanking God, come what may, even in the face of life's temptation to despair and give up in its hardships.

We now have a sharp contrast between "spiritual wisdom" and mere knowledge and even any kind of "human wisdom." Exceeding mere knowledge, spiritual wisdom *welcomes* God's power, including the power of *agapē*, for the sake of living a lasting good life, pleasing to God (or, "worthy of the Lord"). Suppose I know that I cannot save myself if I must meet God's standard of perfect *agapē*, because I have obvious deficiencies on this front. This knowledge of my inadequacy may be genuine knowledge, but it still could be accompanied by a defective volitional attitude of mine toward the reality in question. Suppose I hate that I cannot save myself by God's standard, perhaps because, desiring full autonomy, I strongly wish that I could have saved (and perhaps even created) myself, without any divine help. Perhaps many people share the latter wish, in longing for self-sufficiency or full autonomy, apart from God. In any case, some people testify to their having such a longing.

In Paul's story, the reality that I cannot save myself by God's perfect standard is not hateworthy at all, but is, in fact, good. By this standard, in hating my inadequacy, I hate something good, and this opposes the kind of spiritual wisdom under consideration.

Even a grudging or indifferent reception of something good would be a deficiency in spiritual wisdom. Accordingly, spiritual wisdom, unlike mere knowledge, must be volitionally attuned to what is good in virtue of *welcoming* what is good when the opportunity arises. Such wisdom, then, importantly involves one's will, and hence is not merely intellectual.

We may proceed with the *Oxford English Dictionary* (2nd edn., 1989) characterization of "to welcome": "to receive gladly and hospitably; to accord a friendly reception to." So, if God offered salvation as a good gift to humans, then my wanting to earn my salvation would be misplaced relative to what is good and thus would not fit with spiritual wisdom. God's spiritual wisdom, then, is sensitive to human volition, and if human volition is distorted, the human reception of God's wisdom can be severe, and not casual or easy at all. The volitional attitudes of a potential human recipient can be, in fact, resistant to God's demanding wisdom.

Wisdom and Gethsemane

Paul anchors spiritual wisdom not in an abstract principle or a Platonic Form, but instead in a personal agent who manifests God's power without defect. He refers to "Christ the power of God and the wisdom of God" (1 Cor. 1:24) and to "Christ Jesus who became for us wisdom from God … and redemption" (1 Cor. 1:30). An immediate question concerns what particular features of the person Jesus Christ constitute his being the power and the wisdom of God.

Part of Paul's answer includes the following:

Christ Jesus, who, though he was in the form of God, did not regard equality with God as something to be exploited, but emptied himself, taking the form of a slave, being born in human likeness. And being found in human form, he humbled himself and became obedient to the point of death – even death on a cross. (Phil. 2:5–8)

A key feature is the willing conformity of Jesus to God's will, even when the result is self-sacrificial death. Paul introduces the idea of Jesus's *humble obedience* to God to capture this feature. This obedience differs from *grudging* obedience and even *mere* obedience; it ultimately welcomes God's perfect will, even if one is initially ambivalent and faces rigorous consequences. In his conformity to God's will, Jesus exemplifies the power and wisdom of God as an agent humbly and reverently cooperating with God on the basis of God's distinctive wisdom and power, including the power of self-giving *agapē*.

A striking example of humble cooperation with God appears in the Gospel reports of Jesus in Gethsemane. Mark's Gospel offers the following portrait:

[Jesus and his disciples] went to a place called Gethsemane … He said to them, "I am deeply grieved, even to death …" [H]e threw himself on the ground and prayed that, if it were possible, the hour [of his arrest and crucifixion] might pass from him. He said, "Abba, Father, for you all things are possible; remove this cup [of suffering and death] from me; yet, not what I want, but what you want." (Mark 14:32–36)

This Gethsemane crisis begins with a humanly experienced conflict between a human want and a divine want but ends with a decisive resolution: a human plea by Jesus to God in resolute favor of God's will as a priority. His plea welcomes the fulfillment of God's will as a priority. The proper Gethsemane and human approach to God willingly puts God's perfect will first, even if a serious human want must thereby yield, including a human want to continue earthly life. The consequences of Gethsemane, then, are rigorous by human standards, but we shall see that they bear importantly on human knowledge of a God who is elusive for redemptive purposes.

We now can illuminate Paul's talk of "the message about the cross [of Jesus]" as "the power of God" (1 Cor. 1:18). God's wisdom supplies the power of a lasting good life for humans as an alternative to despair and hence exceeds the value and the power of any wisdom from humans. The heart of God's wisdom is eager conformity to God's perfect will, come what may. Such conformity is exemplified in Jesus Christ, in his Gethsemane attitude of humble obedience to God. This attitude led to his death on a Roman cross, but God, according to Paul, was working in his obedient death to manifest the power of God's self-giving love for wayward humans and eventually to overcome that death. Accordingly, the severe tragedy of Gethsemane and the cross was not an end in itself.

Cruciform wisdom is the kind of spiritual wisdom, from God, shown by Jesus in Gethsemane on his path to the cross. It comes in a person rather than merely a principle, because it inherently involves an engaged personal will, and not just statements or arguments about a will. God's wisdom comes from a personal agent who seeks to engage other personal agents at the level of their wills, where intentional action, interaction, and even *agapē* can emerge. Genuine spiritual wisdom does not reduce to mere talk about such wisdom, because it includes *power* from God to welcome and to obey God's perfect will. Talk is too cheap and easy to supply such powerful wisdom. As a result, Paul finds human wisdom, including the wisdom of the philosophers, to be inadequate for the divine redemption of humans in cooperative life with God.

Cruciform wisdom, according to Paul, is hidden (1 Cor. 2:6–7), because it has a specific redemptive purpose for humans. It aims to engage humans at a level deeper than mere observation, speculation, reflection, or argument. It seeks to encourage a resistant human will to welcome God's self-sacrificial will and to cooperate with it, come what may. Casual inspection or reflection is, accordingly, not a fitting option for human consideration of God's wisdom and power. Instead, this wisdom and its power put humans under a divine challenge to undergo a volitional makeover toward God's perfect will. This makeover calls for our gladly receiving our need of and dependence on God's life-giving power. Such a volitional makeover includes a shift in our priorities regarding power, from selfish power to the power of divine *agapē* as exemplified in Jesus Christ. If we are opposed or indifferent to such a makeover, God may hide divine wisdom and power from us, given that we would not be in a volitional position to receive it aright. Indeed, our not being volitionally present to God may prompt God to refrain from being present in our evidence. God's aim would be to avoid solidifying human resistance to God as long as humans are genuine candidates for redemption.

Personification in Christ

A striking position on the role of Jesus Christ in divine grace and wisdom emerges from Paul, and this position will illuminate our inquiry. The key idea is that God's grace is personified distinctively *in* Jesus. Paul refers to "the grace of God that has been given to you in (*en*) Christ Jesus" (1 Cor. 1:4; cf. Rom. 5:15). This does not seem to be a merely instrumental use of "in," as if the point were simply that the grace of God has been given *by means of* Jesus. Paul does think of God's grace as a gift coming *through*, or by means of, Jesus (see Rom. 5:17), but he has something further in mind. He holds that Jesus Christ himself distinctively personifies God's grace for humans, particularly for their having reconciled life in companionship with God.

Paul summarizes the point as follows: "you know the grace (*charis*) of our Lord Jesus Christ, that though he was rich, yet for your sake he became poor, so that by his poverty you might become rich" (2 Cor. 8:9, RSV). This grace includes Jesus's manifesting God's gracious personal character, particularly in his self-sacrificial death and resurrection (see Phil. 2:5–11). Accordingly, Paul refers to Christ as "the image (*eikōn*) of God" (2 Cor. 4:4; cf. Col. 1:15, 19). If God's personal character motivates actions of divine grace, then the personification of this grace in a human agent who perfectly represents God's moral character can also manifest divine grace.

Even if humans prefer a law or a system of rules as their ultimate guide, God could send a perfect personal agent for a better redemptive effect, in virtue of a direct reflection of God's personal moral character (see 2 Cor. 3:18). This divine option is, in fact, a central part of the New Testament message of redemption. If the divine redemption of humans includes interpersonal divine–human companionship, then God's sending a personal agent would support this goal. A person can enter into genuine companionship with another person but not with concepts, rules, laws, principles, analyses, explanations, or arguments. We shall see how the intended companionship in question brings severity in its wake.

Paul extends his view of the personification of God's grace in Jesus. He refers to "Christ Jesus who became for us wisdom from God, and righteousness and sanctification and redemption" (1 Cor. 1:30; cf. Col. 1:13–14) and to "Christ the power of God and the wisdom of God" (1 Cor. 1:24). The personification of divine redemption in Jesus Christ entails the personification in him of the core features of divine grace, including the gracious divine character and its redemptive power. This fits with Paul's view that divine grace is "in" Jesus, particularly if the key idea is that God's gracious character and its manifestation are found, without moral defect, in Jesus's personal character and his redemptive conduct. Such personification receives inadequate attention in recent philosophy of religion, but we shall correct this shortcoming by identifying the important consequences for religious epistemology and our understanding of divine severity.

Paul contrasts "earthly [or, human] wisdom" and "the grace of God" (2 Cor. 1:12), suggesting that God's grace is central to the "wisdom from/of God" (cf. 1 Cor. 1:24, 30). This suggests the idea of wisdom under the power and authority of divine grace, or (to use an old English verbal form of "grace") wisdom *gracified*. The latter wisdom includes God's redemptive plan as summarized in Paul's "message of the cross" of Jesus (1 Cor. 1:18). This is a message of redemption by the power of God's grace for salvation as reconciled life with God. Divine wisdom, then, operates not by human earning or merit but instead by a divine gift of grace that empowers willing people to live cooperatively and reverently with God.

From Paul's Christian perspective, the cross of Jesus identifies a discomforting limit in human understanding and a severe redemptive act by God. It appears initially to be foolish or at least highly mysterious. Paul remarks: "we proclaim Christ crucified, a stumbling block to Jews and foolishness to Gentiles" (1 Cor. 1:23). In this connection, Paul asks: "Has not God made foolish the wisdom of the world?" (1 Cor. 1:20). In doing so, he echoes Isaiah 29:14: "The wisdom of their wise shall perish, and the discernment of the discerning shall be hidden" (cf. Ps. 33:10). Paul suggests, then, that God aims in the cross of Jesus to deflate any human wisdom that seeks to do without God or God's ways. The target is wisdom that supposedly is humanly sufficient and leaves no room for divine wisdom. God's response is deflationary for redemptive purposes, to save humans from self-destruction in alienation from God.

As suggested, Paul locates wisdom in "Christ the power of God and the wisdom of God" (1 Cor. 1:24). Such personified wisdom from God differs from the theoretical or practical wisdom offered by various philosophers throughout history. This personified wisdom is available as a gift through person-to-person cooperative inter-action with its divine source, but nonpersonified wisdom does not rest on such interaction. Even so, personified wisdom from God is no panacea for all of our questions about God's ways.

The wisdom from God now available to humans leaves many troubling questions unanswered, thus highlighting the discom-forting incompleteness of such wisdom. For instance, our lack of a comprehensive theodicy for God's allowing evil, as indicated by the book of Job (see chaps. 38–41), makes this limitation obvious but still troubling for many inquirers. Even if we have personified wisdom from God, we still remain in the dark about some questions about God's specific purposes for evil in the world. Arguably, we should have expected this limitation, after reflection on our highly limited understanding of God's purposes in general. Nonetheless, as we shall see, such limited understanding regarding life's evil and severity does not preclude a human life reconciled to God on the basis of salient evidence of a kind to be characterized.

In Paul's understanding, "the message of the cross" of Jesus calls for a careful revaluing of human attitudes and expectations about God. It invites us to conceive of God as not always protecting people, even obedient people, from suffering and death, but instead as mani-festing human suffering and death as redeemable by God on divine terms. This message implies that human corrective power over evil faces discomforting limits, beyond the real limits on human under-standing regarding evil. The limits on human power, however, need not entail despair over human suffering and death, particularly if God empowers the resurrection of humans after their death, instead of rescuing them in a way that avoids suffering and death. This book contends, accordingly, that divine severity does not support human despair. It identifies a trustworthy basis for human hope in God, an interactive God, as an alternative to unyielding despair.

Given a gracious God, the limits of wisdom available to humans would stem, at least in part, from severe divine grace. Such wisdom would be a divine gift, given on God's perfect (if severe) terms, for the sake of manifesting God's moral character in humans and thereby improving human moral character in companionship with God. In virtue of receiving this gift, humans would be capable of personifying divine wisdom in their lives, if imperfectly and intermittently. The source of wisdom for humans in a gift of divine grace would undermine the supposed legitimacy of any human boasting in the wisdom available to humans (see 1 Cor. 1:28–31). We cannot plausibly take self-credit for a gift not of our own making or earning.

As we shall see, the gift of divine grace, when received, is inherently person-to-person, agent-to-agent companionship, including cooperative fellowship, and is therefore irreducible to nonpersonal phenomena, such as concepts, principles, and arguments. Søren Kierkegaard moves in the right direction with his remark about God that "the helper is the help" (1850, p. 15), thus suggesting that the gift-giver is the gift. In Paul's language, the gift of grace includes a gracious divine call of humans into a life of companionship or fellowship (*koinōnia*) with God and his Son, Jesus Christ (1 Cor. 1:9; cf. 1 John 1:2–3). Wisdom gracified, we shall see, includes genuine (if limited) understanding regarding the good life anchored in divine grace as companionship with God. Developing this neglected approach to wisdom, this book identifies its bearing on some central questions regarding divine severity in the redemption of humans.

EXPECTING A SEVERE GOD

Being perfectly active in gracious righteousness, God would oppose whatever obstructs perfect righteousness among agents. This opposition would be wisely intentional and not impulsive or irrational, and it could be severe in human life. It could allow, however, for some short-term unrighteousness for the sake of long-term righteousness. So, God's active opposition to certain occurrences of unrighteousness, such as unjust human warfare, could be eventual rather than immediate. God could allow some episodes of unrighteousness to persist for a while in order to have them culminate and be seen as harmful by a wide audience. In other words, God could be patient toward some unrighteousness, in order to enhance the redemption of humans.

A sound morality would not require God actively to oppose all unrighteousness immediately if a purpose of greater righteousness would be served only by means of postponing active opposition. Opposition to unrighteousness, then, does not entail immediate active opposition to all unrighteousness. The relevant notion of "greater" righteousness is complicated, of course, but we need not digress.

Biblical severity

The New Testament offers some ascriptions of severity to God, and they can illuminate how God can be oppositional. In Luke's version of the Parable of the Pounds, Jesus attributes the following statement to a man who functions as God's approved representative and thus images Jesus himself and even God: "You knew that I was a severe (*austēros*) man, taking up what I lay down and reaping what I did not sow" (Luke 19:22, RSV; cf. Matt. 25:24). Likewise, Paul remarks as follows, in connection with the divine offer of mercy to humans coupled with the divine judgment on human resistance: "See then the kindness and the severity (*apotomian*) of God" (Rom. 11:22, RSV). Evidently, then, some of the New Testament writers would propose that divine righteous love (*agapē*) has a certain severity about it.

We can use the previous *OED* definition to clarify the talk of divine severity in Luke and Paul. We begin with the idea that divine severity involves "strictness or sternness in dealing with others; stern or rigorous disposition or behaviour; rigour in treatment, discipline, punishment, or the like." We need to clarify this talk of severity to capture a fruitful conception of God often ignored by philosophers, theologians, and other reflective people. This neglected conception prevents us from thinking of God as akin to a doting grandparent or a celestial Santa Claus figure. The neglected conception rightly preserves genuine moral *gravitas*, particularly righteousness, in God and in God's vigorous dealings with humans.

Since the time of Dietrich Bonhoeffer's work on discipleship (1937), many people have been wary of "cheap grace" from God. Such grace would not challenge its recipients to undergo profound transformation toward righteousness corresponding to God's moral character. According to Paul, in contrast, the divine gift of grace includes the gift of righteousness and is therefore profoundly morally transformative (see Rom. 5:17). In Paul's view, God's redemptive plan is that "grace might reign through [the gift of] righteousness to eternal life" (Rom. 5:21, RSV). Given this key linking of grace and righteousness, we should be suspicious of any "cheap theism" that either makes God morally lax toward unrighteousness or divorces divine grace from divinely empowered righteousness among humans. If severity is a divine meta-attribute that applies to the divine attribute of righteousness (among other divine attributes), such cheap theism will misrepresent God's moral character. Even if the latter theism gives us a god, it does not yield a morally perfect God who is worthy of worship.

Theologians and philosophers of religion speak often of divine "love," but they talk much less frequently, if at all, of divine severity toward unrighteousness. The result is a conception of a God who is alleged to be "loving," in some sense, but who is anything but a "consuming fire" of moral righteousness (see Deut. 4:24; Heb. 12:29; cf. Knight 1959, pp. 273–281). This conception sacrifices divine righteousness for a kind of love that is soft on unrighteousness. We shall ask whether this conception does justice to the moral character of a God worthy of worship. Arguably, divine love involving worthiness of worship would be severely righteous in a way that rigorously opposes unrighteousness of any kind. If so, God would be actively *oppositional* and perhaps even *severely* oppositional toward unrighteousness, in keeping with God's redemptive wisdom. This book finds a divine redemptive goal of the moral transformation of humans in such oppositional behavior and explains its bearing on human interaction with God.

Many biblical passages yield a striking portrait of a severely oppositional God. In the Hebrew Bible, God is portrayed as inherently jealous: "you shall worship no other god, because the Lord, whose name is Jealous, is a jealous God" (Exod. 34:14; cf. Deut. 6:14–15). This divine jealousy differs from, and is even incompatible with, selfish human jealousy. The rigorous jealousy in Israel's God aims to protect the people of Israel in their relationship with God by opposing all idolatrous substitutes, visible or invisible. Accordingly, this God announces to the wayward people of Israel: "I will chastise you in just measure, and I will by no means leave you unpunished" (Jer. 30:11; cf. Exod. 20:5). God intends such just chastisement to be corrective and life-giving, according to Jeremiah and other Hebrew prophets; so, it is not an end in itself. Even so, as punishment, it can be retributive, or compensatory, in virtue of penalizing behavior opposed to God's perfect character and life. The same holds for the notorious divine wrath that motivates the prophesied punishment of people disobeying God; it, too, can offer a penalty as well as a purported correction. A penalty could include, for instance, severe human discomfort or stress intended to draw attention to a needed correction among wayward humans.

The New Testament portrays God as oppositional toward unrighteousness in a number of ways. Paul writes: "The wrath of God is revealed from heaven against all ungodliness and wickedness of those who by their wickedness suppress the truth" (Rom. 1:18). He also remarks: "the creation was subjected to futility, not of its own will but by the will of the one [namely, God] who subjected it, in hope that the creation itself will be set free from its bondage to decay and will obtain the freedom of the glory of the children of God" (Rom. 8:20–21).

The divine aim, or hope, is to free people from bondage to what does not give a life of freedom with God. Pursuing this aim, God subjects creation to futility, according to Paul, in order to manifest and to overcome the inadequacy of the created world for the life of freedom needed by humans. The New Testament message implies that God alone will emerge as adequate for providing such life. Paul suggests that God intends tribulation in human life to produce human character and hope agreeable to God's character and life (Rom. 5:3–5). Tribulation in human life, then, is not portrayed as an end in itself; it stems from a divine aim for the redemption of humans in cooperative life with God.

Another way to oppose unrighteousness includes God's supplying receptive humans with a special kind of power. This is the power to "put to death the [disobedient] deeds of the body" that alienate people from the life of freedom with God (see Rom. 8:13). In this view, humans need help, particularly helpful power, from God to overcome the world's pull toward unrighteousness. The helpful power would be an antidote, at least for willing humans, to unrighteousness as disobedience toward God. Divine opposition to human unrighteousness, accordingly, would aim for a human life of freedom reconciled to God. This book explores what such a life entails and thereby illuminates divine severity as a redemptive cause.

Divine opposition to human unrighteousness has various manifestations and resists any simple characterization. It includes the divine severity of subjecting creation to futility, or frustration, in order to liberate people from their bondage to decay in inadequate sources of freedom and security. Such divine opposition occurs in at least some human suffering, dying, and death, but an important qualification is needed. God could subject creation to futility, for redemptive purposes, without *directly* bringing about every instance of futility in creation.

God could create free agents who freely bring about some of the world's futility and are therefore causally and morally responsible for it. This option can raise serious problems for a characterization of God as successful in realizing God's perfect will at every point. The latter characterization would have to face the reality of the power of created free agents, if they exist, to frustrate God's perfect will. Obviously, some agents do not comply with God's perfect will. Part of God's noncoercive "providence," then, may be to allow some created agents to exercise control, even harmful control, over parts of creation. God would not have to be the direct cause of all that occurs in creation, because God could allow some opposition to unrighteousness to arise from the causal powers of created agents. In that case, God's *permissive will* would be operating, even if God's perfect *executive will* would not. God's allowing an action by another agent does not entail God's causing, performing, recommending, or approving that action.

A particularly memorable case of severity emerges in the crucifixion of Jesus Christ as a self-avowed emissary for God. Aside from the theological significance of his crucifixion, the human treatment of Jesus just before his death was remarkably severe. Some theologians assign this severe treatment ultimately to God, and not just to the Roman officials and soldiers, on the ground that God chose to punish Jesus to save humans from the just deserts of their sins. This interpretation is highly controversial, partly because it lacks clear support in the New Testament, and, in any case, it raises serious questions about divine justice. Nonetheless, God's *allowing* the crucifixion of Jesus is severe by any ordinary standard of severe permission, even if certain Roman officials and soldiers were causally and morally responsible for the harsh punishment involved. Accordingly, the New Testament invites us to face a kind of divine severity.

The God of the Hebrew Bible sometimes judges people by withdrawing the divine presence from them. God reports to Moses: "My anger will be kindled against them [the people of Israel] in that day. I will forsake them and hide my face from them; they will become easy prey, and many terrible troubles will come upon them" (Deut. 31:17). In such a case, divine hiding involves severe divine punishment, even if the recipients are unaware of the punishment. (It does not follow that all divine hiding entails God's punishment of humans; see Moser 2008.)

Some commentators (for instance, Ward 1964, p. 51) apply the idea of divine hiding to Jesus's cry of abandonment on the cross: "My God, my God, why have you forsaken me?" (Mark 15:34; cf. Ps. 22:1, Matt. 27:46). The idea is that, in order to condemn human sin, God withdrew the divine presence and fellowship from Jesus, as the atoning representative of humans, at the time of his troubled cry to God. This is arguably a plausible way to unpack Paul's following remark: "God has done what the law, weakened by the flesh, could not do: by sending his own Son in the likeness of sinful flesh, and to deal with sin, he condemned sin in the flesh" (Rom. 8:3). It does not follow, however, that in condemning "sin in the flesh" God condemned Jesus himself. The message of Paul is that God ratified Jesus and his obedient life by resurrecting him, but only after allowing a severe death by crucifixion. This message offers Jesus as a personal model of human dying into lasting life with God. (Chapters 3 and 4 return to the relevant notion of dying into life with God.)

Three questions can illuminate the potential ways of God toward humans. These questions may be called *expectation-evoking*, because they are helpful in eliciting sound human expectations regarding God and God's ways of intervention in human lives. Human inquiry about God would gain enhanced precision if humans gave more attention to such questions. The familiar obscurity in human inquiry about God suggests that we should attend carefully to such questions. In particular, philosophers and theologians have given inadequate attention to expectation-evoking questions about God in connection with the problem of divine severity. This book begins to correct that deficiency, as it uses abductive considerations of explanatory power to assess proposed answers. Many people have misguided expectations about God, given God's worthiness of worship, and therefore they would benefit from questions that prompt careful reflection on these expectations.

Personalism

The first question for improving our expectations of God is this: how should we expect God, being worthy of worship, to relate to humans if God aims to be known directly by them *as a personal agent*, and not as a principle, an idea, or an impersonal cause? If God is worthy of worship, then God is a morally perfect, perfectly loving agent and therefore is personal rather than nonpersonal. In virtue of being personal, God would be an *intentional* agent, with purposes and plans, and God's being personal could be reflected, if vaguely at times, in human persons. Accordingly, God could not be replaced without loss by a principle, an idea, or an impersonal cause. Any such replacement would dispense with perfect *agapē*, for instance, because only a personal agent can offer perfect *agapē*. Principles, ideas, and impersonal causes do not love anything, or perform any intentional actions, for that matter. The god of Aristotle, for instance, arguably faces trouble on this front. It is unclear, in any case, that his god is robustly personal as one who cares about others.

Direct knowledge of God as a personal agent with a will would serve an important redemptive purpose. It would give humans a direct apprehension of God that could not be supplied by principles, ideas, or impersonal causes. In doing so, it would reveal God's irreducibly personal character in a way that principles, ideas, or impersonal causes could not. Such direct knowledge thereby would convey an important feature of God's actual character to humans and could be an experiential avenue to awareness of God as worthy of worship and perfectly loving. In addition, it could anchor ongoing volitional companionship with God. It would offer a significant contrast with an unduly abstract conception of God.

Aiming to be known directly as a personal agent, God would value *interpersonal interaction* of a direct, second-person sort. Such interpersonality is *de re*, or more accurately *de te* (from the Latin "tu" = "you"), involving the direct acquaintance of one personal agent with another personal agent in the second person, beyond any *de dicto* (conceptual or notional) relation involving ideas or principles. This kind of acquaintance between God and humans is not bodily acquaintance, because God has no physical body. (Likewise, our acquaintance with other human persons, as persons, has less to do with physical bodies than we might think, because personality is not inherently corporeal.) We should look elsewhere, then, for a context for such direct interpersonal acquaintance.

The most plausible human context for direct acquaintance with God is human *conscience*. This is the psychological place where a human could directly know, and be known, together with God (see the etymology of "*con* + *scientia*") as God calls a person (sometimes, to account) in the second person, as *you*. This proposal fits with Paul's suggestion that in human conscience God bears witness to the divine moral character as represented in the law of God, thereby holding people accountable (Rom. 2:14–15). It also fits with his suggestion that his conscience can confirm something by God's Spirit (Rom. 9:1; cf. 2 Cor. 1:12, 5:11). In this perspective, one's conscience is the inner place, involving one's spiritual "heart," where one can directly experience hearing from, being called by, or being taught by God (see John 6:45, Matt. 16:17, 1 Cor. 1:9, 1 Thess. 3:11, 4:7, 9, Heb. 3:7, 15). Arguably, this perspective underlies Paul's remark to the Corinthian Christians that "the testimony of Christ was confirmed in you" (1 Cor. 1:6, KJV).

The role of human conscience in knowledge of God is widely neglected among contemporary philosophers, and this neglect can obscure the experiential reality of the God of Abraham, Isaac, Jacob, and Jesus. It also can minimize the crucial role of human prayer in evidence-conferring interaction with this God, because such prayer ideally stems from conscience. Human prayer to God finds its perfect model in the prayer of Jesus to God in Gethsemane: "Father, not what I will, but what You will" (Mark 14:36). This book contends that such a Gethsemane attitude toward the priority of God's will is central not only to cooperative life with God but also to human appropriation of salient evidence for God. This approach is neglected among philosophers of religion, past and present, but this book begins to correct this neglect.

Our first expectation-invoking question leads to a subsidiary question: is there actually a Godward presence or call in human conscience? Human conscience can be insensitive, corrupted, and outright diabolical. We should be very skeptical, then, of Wittgenstein's following remark in his *Notebooks*: "Certainly it is correct to say: Conscience is the voice of God" (1916, p. 75). Even so, conscience is not thereby emptied of Godward value, just as perception does not lose its evidential or cognitive value given the various misleading functions or uses of perception.

Humans can treat conscience honestly or dishonestly, and earnestly or indifferently. Dishonest or indifferent treatment of conscience does not undermine the representational value of conscience treated honestly or earnestly. Personal accountability thus can figure importantly in the handling of human conscience, including in its representing or not representing God to oneself. In addition, we should not expect conscience to coerce humans in its representing God, as if humans had no responsible interactive role toward God. This book develops this important topic constructively, while avoiding Wittgenstein's extreme position.

Many philosophers of religion seek principles that supply intricate human explanations of God's ways. This book argues, however, that we have to deal primarily with a personal God who may not honor such principles (cf. 1 Cor. 1:18–25). As a result, we should expect our characterizations of God in some areas to be less "cut and dried" and even less adequate than we might have wished. Even so, I shall contend that God can, and does, make Godself known via a receptive human conscience in ways that are much more personally challenging (even severe) and morally robust than the philosophical arguments of, for instance, traditional natural theology.

We shall see that a distinctive kind of personifying evidence of God can be found in the personal moral character of a human agent, beyond mere propositions, claims, or arguments. For instance, John's Gospel and Paul's letters suggest that Jesus Christ is the perfect human personifying evidence of God, and he is, of course, not a mere proposition, claim, or argument. As a personal agent, with definite intentions and plans, he can serve as personifying evidence for God, who also has definite intentions and plans of the same sort. Arguably, other humans, too, can become personifying evidence of God in virtue of their cooperatively receiving certain features of God's moral character. In this approach, involving evidential personalism, persons can play a role in foundational evidence of God that cannot be reduced to mere propositions, claims, or arguments.

Looking for principles rather than persons as ultimate, some philosophers of religion miss the distinctive point and value of evidential personalism regarding God. For instance, much of analytic philosophy of religion fails to consider some of the key features of Jewish–Christian theistic personalism, such as the bearing of Jesus Christ himself on human evidence and knowledge of God. This book contends that we would do well not to sacrifice such personalism for any kind of deism, mere theism, or principle-based approach to God. Instead, we should be receptive to the salient evidence of God as it comes to us, in its suitable form.

Deep transformation

Our second expectation-evoking question is this: how should we expect God to act in relation to humans if God aims to redeem them not just as thinkers but as *morally responsible volitional agents* who need a self-commitment to cooperation with God, for the sake of companionship with God? We may formulate the latter aim in terms of God's aiming to win humans, themselves, and not just arguments with humans. This divine aim would offer a gift of divine–human reconciliation that originates outside any human resources. It would include a person-to-person (divine-to-human) call to be renewed at one's motivational center via a life of self-commitment to cooperation with God. Such a divine aim would feature (a) the divine generosity of companionship offered to humans and, by way of an accountable response, (b) the human cooperation demanded by God. Notoriously, the latter demand can lead to real severity in cases of human irresponsibility toward God, because God would call for the end of anti-God human ways.

From God's side, the companionship would include God's self-giving intervention in Jesus Christ on behalf of humans, whereby God seeks to self-identify and live with humans. Without such divine grace in action, many humans properly would doubt that they meet the standard set by God's own moral character, and they therefore would lack proper confidence regarding their acceptance by God. As a result, without divine grace in action, any self-commitment to God would be seriously deficient. This book explores the aims of redemptive divine companionship to illuminate divine grace and its severity.

God's redemptive aim would be to give cooperative humans a renewed volitional center of agency in companionship with God, including a renewed will to live agreeably and therefore unselfishly with God. The divine aim of human companionship with God would stem from the human need of such benefits as encouragement, chastisement, and specific personal guidance from God. It also would stem from the human need of seeking, including asking for, these benefits from God, as part of interpersonal communion. As a result, no mere concept, principle, command, law, morality, argument, or human effort would accomplish this redemptive aim.

The transformation of humans in divine redemption would oppose moral self-sufficiency in humans. Accordingly, it would oppose any presumption of humans being good *on their own*. Instead, it would aim for moral transformation *in human companionship with God*. For the good of humans, this would be reverent, submissive transformation anchored in the prayer offered by Jesus to God in Gethsemane: "Father, not what I will, but what You will." Such transformation would be person-to-person, in a context where a human submits to God in companionship with God. The result would be significant human change via willing human participation in God's perfect moral character. This book explores the nature and aims of such participation, including the bearing of divine severity on it.

God's pursuit of the volitional transformation of humans would not be served by just abstract theoretical claims about God, such as claims about divine impassibility or divine omniscience. Claims of that sort would invite philosophical and theological discussion, perhaps even endlessly, but they would not challenge the volitional center of an agent. They would not challenge an agent to make a commitment of self-sacrificial love to a God of redemptive grace. Concrete self-sacrificial actions and corresponding commands from God, in contrast, could infuse the needed challenge with motivational significance for humans. Accordingly, the Christian message is that God's culminating revelation comes in the self-giving and demanding person and life of Jesus Christ, who manifests God's grace and wisdom, and not just in ideas or arguments about God.

We shall ask what the relevant divine actions and commands would look like, given God's perfect character that includes divine severity. We shall see that the separation of (evidence for) God's existence from (evidence for) God's perfect personal agency, as in much natural theology, invites serious problems and should therefore be avoided. This book identifies a role for human self-sacrifice, of the sort immortalized in the crisis of Gethsemane, as part of a proper response to divine self-sacrifice. It argues that a philosophy of religion adequate to a God worthy of worship must award a key role to human self-sacrifice to God, after the model of Gethsemane.

Specifically, it contends that suitable faith in God includes a distinctive kind of self-sacrifice to God.

Human boasting undone

Our third expectation-evoking question is this: how should we expect a God worthy of worship to intervene in human lives if this God seeks to undermine all selfish or otherwise misguided human boasting? One plausible answer is straightforward: by an undeserved gift of divine grace that displaces any such boasting. This displacement of human boasting would challenge misguided human self-pride on various fronts, including in connection with morality, knowledge, and wisdom. Such pride involves one's exaggerated assessment of oneself or of one's contributions or achievements, such as when one self-confidently takes credit for something (for instance, in morality, knowledge, or wisdom) where such credit is manifestly not due.

A familiar example includes a human's self-confidently taking credit for what is plainly an undeserved gift. If wisdom, righteousness, and life from God, for instance, are undeserved gifts to humans, then humans are in no position to take credit for these gifts. Misguided human pride regarding such gifts is harmful, because it disallows God, from a specific human perspective, to be truly gracious in some central areas of human existence. Substituting human self-credit for divine grace, such pride obscures the importance of human dependence on a gracious, morally perfect God.

Because human agency is a requirement for divine companionship with humans, we should not expect divine grace to coerce a human response of commitment to life with God. Owing to moral weakness, however, humans cannot live up to God's moral character by themselves. They therefore fall short of perfectly obeying divine commands to love God fully and to love others unselfishly. In manifesting this human moral inadequacy, divine love-commands show the human need for divine grace, for God's mercy and forgiveness toward humans. (On the New Testament role of those commands, see Furnish 1972.) They show that humans do not merit, or earn, approval from God, if God's perfect moral character sets the standard for approval. Human moral pride will not welcome this lesson, but this is no count against the lesson. Instead, such pride itself falls under proper suspicion once the reality of human moral deficiency emerges. This deficiency does not entail despair, however, if divine mercy underwrites the offer of unearned forgiveness to humans.

Divine moral perfection combined with human moral imperfection, including human self-pride and despair, would call for a rigorous human struggle in receiving divine grace and wisdom. Following Pascal (*Pensées*, sec. 435), we shall see that neither human self-pride nor human despair would enjoy a firm footing relative to a severe God's moral character. If divine grace and wisdom, as personified in Jesus Christ crucified, encompass redemptive self-sacrifice for God's purpose, then human appropriation of such grace and wisdom will be not only a response to, but also an exemplification of, such sacrifice. This appropriation will go against any human self-pride or despair incompatible with such sacrifice. It will involve, as a fitting response, self-sacrificial appropriation of grace and wisdom which are likewise self-sacrificial.

Method

This book uses expectation-evoking questions to focus on human expectations for God's reality, while offering the term "God" as a preeminent title requiring worthiness of worship. It contends that our understanding of evidence, and thus of knowledge, regarding

God should be guided by the relevant notion of a God worthy of worship, rather than by any cognitive standard that is questionable relative to this notion. Our initial question becomes not so much whether God exists as what the character and purposes of a God worthy of worship would be, if God exists. In keeping with the previous expectation-evoking questions, we should ask this: what *kind* of evidence and knowledge of God's reality should we expect a God worthy of worship to offer to humans? A plausible answer is that God would offer the kind of evidence and knowledge that represents and advances God's worship-worthy moral character among humans, including God's corresponding redemptive purposes.

Arguably, we should expect evidence and knowledge of divine reality to be available to humans only in a manner suitable to divine *purposes* in self-revelation. We should expect these divine purposes to include the redemptive transformation of human moral characters toward God's moral character, for the sake of human improvement in companionship with God. This lesson yields a major shift in our understanding of human knowledge and evidence of divine reality. It demands that inquirers become sensitive to the character and purposes of a God worthy of worship, in a manner that challenges and reorients human wills. This lesson will illuminate some of the severity in God and in human life, in terms of the needed volitional transformation of humans in companionship with God. (In this area, the book extends an epistemological lesson of Moser 2008, 2010a.)

Some philosophers think of religious faith as purely intellectual, similar to belief that, for instance, transfinite cardinal numbers or subatomic leptons exist. This, however, is a big mistake that leads to confusions about what kind of evidence is to be expected for religious faith in God. We shall see that the relevant evidence is to be appropriated in a self-sacrificial struggle in response to a divine challenge to humans. In particular, we need a characterization of religious faith in God in terms of a human moral struggle to appropriate divine grace and wisdom, for the sake of reverent companionship with God. (Chapters 2 and 3 return to this theme.)

Our inquiry about divine severity does not reduce to an inquiry about a traditional problem of evil, because the reality of divine severity is no challenge to God's existence or even God's goodness. On the contrary, one should expect divine severity upon reflection about the implications of the worthiness of worship suited to God. Even so, one might propose that divine severity is a challenge to God's graciousness, on the ground that it suggests that God is holding back on the best for humans even if God is morally good. A natural question, then, is this: could not God be more gracious and less severe, without any loss of value? In other words, could not God's "good and perfect will" (Rom. 12:2) be less severe? More specifically, is God at best restrictedly gracious toward at least some people? We shall face these difficult questions after characterizing divine severity in some detail, particularly with regard to its underlying redemptive purposes.

A key conclusion will be that divine severity, properly understood, does not undermine perfect divine grace but should be expected in the light of such grace. A resilient, redemptive understanding of divine severity, given the standard of worthiness of worship, will emerge from our expectation-evoking questions regarding divine purposes. Some of the human frustration with divine severity will fall away in the proper context of illumination. This "proper context," however, may not be cheap and easy, but may instead involve a particular kind of encounter with a God worthy of worship. We are, in any case, unable to rule out such an option at the start.

Severity and flux

Infinite humbling and grace, and then a struggling born of
gratitude – this is Christianity.

(Kierkegaard 1851b, p. 434)

Christianity ... in its philosophical stance ... takes the bull of
impermanence [including time, body, and history] by the horns
and shakes it into permanence.

(Smith 1970, p. 171)

What, if anything, is the bearing of the flux, or impermanence, of this
world on a commitment to the severe God of Jewish and Christian
theism? This chapter contends that the bearing is positive rather
than negative, given the redemptive character and aims of this mysterious God. It proposes that a distinctive *agapē* struggle involving
humans and God is an elusive indicator of permanence in connection
with this redemptive God. Philosophers of religion typically have
neglected this important lesson, often as a result of looking for permanence in the wrong places. We shall identify the upshot of this
lesson for the available evidence for God. This chapter offers a broad
vision of such evidence on the basis of plausibility considerations,
and this vision opens up some new prospects in the philosophy of
religion, particularly in connection with divine severity and human
evidence for God.

FLUX IN LIFE

We all have various experiences as we read a sentence on a page, for instance, and we have various experiences prior to reading the sentence and after reading it. Many, if not all, of these experiences are transitory, but some of them are nonetheless salient, even strikingly salient, such as our hearing a screaming police siren or a roaring jet engine. My world of experience – like that of many other people, I suspect – seems to be largely in motion rather than static. This world of experience can become tiring and exhausting in all of its ongoing movement, and such movement can be confusing and even psychologically overwhelming for some people. Even so, change can be for the good; it need not be bad for humans.

If some things in my world of experience persist for a while, my overall world of experience is certainly not immutable or even unchanging. It features ongoing changes of various sorts: in color, brightness, sound, taste, texture, and so on. In fact, changes highlight not only the objects I apparently experience but also my subjective experiential states. On both sides, subjectively and objectively, things apparently come and go, sometimes without any apparent rhyme or reason. Indeed, the occurrence of changes may be the only thing that does not seem to change in my world of experience. Even if flux does not reign fully in the end, it seems to take the lion's share of my world of experience, and it often contributes to harmful severity in human life.

We naturally might wonder whether *any* part of my experience is beyond flux, in virtue of its enduring through and beyond the flux. More significantly, can my life itself endure, with or without the kind of ongoing change I frequently experience? Even more to the point, *will* my life endure amidst all of the surrounding change? Or, instead, will my life go down in dissolution with all of life's passing energies? Is everything crumbling in our midst, accompanied by our own eventual demise? Clearly, no easy answer, let alone a consensus, is at hand, especially among philosophers. Such difficult questions can occupy a person for a lifetime, through many experienced changes of various sorts, and they may even turn one into a philosopher of some sort. Even so, enduring answers tend to be elusive, even for inquirers who retreat to philosophy.

Ongoing flux marks not only my experiences but also my thoughts and motives, including my desires and intentions. My thoughts change with varying degrees of speed, and likewise for my motives. Sometimes my thoughts do not yield to silence, and the inner noise of insomnia results. At times, furthermore, my thoughts revolve around a philosophical question, and their movement makes perceived time race ahead for me. An hour passes in an apparent minute, and I find myself late for an appointment, having failed to remember other significant thoughts. I think one thing and then another, in rapid succession, and the pattern continues through my life. My desires and emotions sometimes follow suit, and I do not seem to be in full control of the ongoing movement. Every bit of short-lived relief from change seems to be followed by another experienced disturbance or at least another problem or question. Who will rescue us from this turbulent world of flux and tribulation? Will we all finally perish in its motion-riddled mix? Meanwhile, in any case, flux often increases the bad severity in our fragile lives.

Happily or unhappily, many people fail to acknowledge the flux around us, perhaps as a result of distraction by a familiar diversion (such as a sport or a hobby) or as a result of latching on to something that seems relatively stable (such as another person or a consistent mental or behavioral routine). What people look for or attend to in the flux can influence how they apprehend the flux, whether vaguely or clearly. Suppose that, in the tradition of Plato, we are looking for something immutable that transcends, and is "separate from," the flux, such as the abstract Idea or Form of Goodness. Alternatively, in the subsequent tradition of Aristotle, we might look for something immutable within the flux, such as the enmattered Form or Essence of Beauty inhabiting some physical objects. In either case, we would be looking for something that is not subject to change and therefore can contribute some stability for us in our world of ongoing flux.

Even if we found such a source of stability as an Idea or Form, we would need to ask whether and how the prospective stability could become internal to us humans and thus stabilize our actual experience. Clearly, anything immutable in the manner sought by Plato and Aristotle would not be personal in any familiar sense of "personal." Anything personal in a familiar sense would be, at least in principle, susceptible to change in intentional interaction with other persons, perhaps as an intended result of communication with persons. The Forms of Plato and Aristotle, regardless of their differences relative to the material world, are not susceptible to any such change; they have no intentions, good or bad, and hence are not persons. (For relevant details on Plato and Aristotle on permanence, see Hintikka 1967.)

In launching Western philosophy, Plato and Aristotle sought a kind of stability, at least as a basis for durable truth, in the presence of life's flux. We might wonder if they were looking for some kind of *security* for human inquirers in the flux, that is, stable support against the dissolution of inquirers (as inquiring souls) in the flux. The issue is whether their postulating the immutable objects of speculative metaphysics, such as Ideas or Forms, sought a desired escape from the wide-ranging flux in our world of experience. In particular, was the desired escape in question an intended release of *us, ourselves,* from the flux to the extent that we somehow participate in the immutable Ideas or Forms? I suspect so, given the Platonic ideal (however wavering) of philosophy as salvific for qualified humans.

Plato's intended kind of participation in the Forms is arguably intellectual. Even so, he evidently offers it (particularly in *Phaedo*, 105c–107b) as an avenue of salvation or survival (even with flourishing) for human souls that suitably participate in the immutable and imperishable Forms. Perhaps we ourselves, as intellectually enlightened souls, can persist despite the surrounding flux, in virtue of our participating in the stable, imperishable Forms. Although Plato is not consistently clear on this redemptive story, such a story offers a plausible diagnosis of his approach in the *Phaedo* and the *Republic* to human participation in the immutable and imperishable Forms (see *Republic*, 608c–612a, on the immortality of the soul; cf. *Timaeus*, 90a–d).

Let's suppose that we actually could have the kind of intellectual apprehension of immutable Forms acknowledged by Plato and Aristotle. What exactly would this gain for us? Or, more easily, what would it fail to gain for us? It is doubtful that it would gain lasting survival for us, whatever else it gains. Our own apprehension of the immutable Forms could come and go, even willy-nilly, and it therefore would fail to transfer, at least automatically, the immutability or the imperishability of the Forms to us as transitory souls. As long as our apprehension of the Ideas would be subject to temporal fluctuation, our survival as stable souls would be thus subject too, at least apart from some further considerations about the transference of imperishability.

It is doubtful that our apprehension of the immutable Forms, as endorsed by Plato and Aristotle, would gain moral perfection or even considerable moral improvement for us. Our selfish tendencies could persist and even increase despite our apprehension of the Forms, however morally demanding the latter are. At least early on, Plato had hoped, and even boldly assumed, that one's suitable acquaintance with the Forms would direct one's will to become morally sound in virtue of conforming to the Form of the Good.

Plato's hope appears to be wishful thinking at best, given the reality of human weakness of will, or what Aristotle called *akrasia*. In particular, I can know what is good, including the Form of the Good, but still fail to will what is good, perhaps as a result of my selfish intentions conflicting with what is good. On reflection, we all can identify with such a predicament of moral failure where the shortcoming is volitional and not merely cognitive. Accordingly, Plato has found very few followers in this area, and Aristotle has prevailed regarding the question of *akrasia*. Even so, we still need an antidote to the flux that threatens us as enduring agents and adds to life's harmful severity.

Some philosophers have boldly recommended against any proposed ideal of our surviving as enduring agents without end. For instance, Bernard Williams has claimed that "an endless life would be a meaningless one ... There is no desirable or significant property which life would have more of, or have more unqualifiedly, if we lasted forever" (1973, p. 89). He adds:

Nothing less would do for eternity than something that makes [human] boredom *unthinkable*. What could that be? Something that could be guaranteed to be at every moment utterly absorbing? But if a man has and retains a character, there is no reason to suppose that there is anything that could be that. (1973, p. 95)

This dismissal of the value of lasting human survival is much too quick, and implausibly bold too.

We have no reason to hold that human boredom must be *unthinkable*. On the contrary, it seems adequate that human boredom is in fact permanently out of place in a lasting life. The stronger modal requirement, suggested by Williams, is excessive, because the mere thinkability of boredom does not make it an actual threat to the lasting meaningful survival of humans.

Williams gives no real challenge to a plausible theistic view that divine–human companionship or fellowship can serve as a "significant property which life would have more of, or have more unqualifiedly, if we lasted forever." The increase of such companionship could offer ever-deepening meaning in lasting human life and therefore an ever-present alternative to human boredom. Until we can eliminate or at least defeat this option, we cannot endorse with any cogency the pessimism of Williams. Williams himself offers no good reason to disregard this plausible option.

Thomas Nagel recommends the absurdity of human life, including lasting human life, on the basis of "the perpetual possibility of regarding everything about which we are serious as arbitrary, or open to doubt" (1971, p. 153). He explains:

We see ourselves from outside, and all the contingency and specificity of our aims and pursuits become clear. Yet when we take this view and recognize what we do as arbitrary, it does not disengage us from life, and there lies our absurdity: not in the fact that such an external view can be taken of us, but in the fact that we ourselves can take it, without ceasing to be the persons whose ultimate concerns are so coolly regarded. (1971, p. 155)

This modal consideration, involving a view that we *can* take, underlies Nagel's view of life's absurdity.

Nagel makes a mistake analogous to the error just ascribed to Williams. The mere *imagination* of a purely external viewpoint on human life does not yield what is factual or even what is probably factual regarding human life. It therefore does not yield anything actually or even probably absurd about human life. If an external viewpoint devoid of ultimate purposes were arguably factual, one might have the makings of a case for the absurdity of a human life presumed to have real purpose.

Nagel does not show that his imagined external viewpoint is factual. Instead, he settles for a dubious modal inference: "If we can step back from the purposes of individual life and doubt their point, we can step back also from … the kingdom, power, and glory of

God, and put all these things into question in the same way" (1971, p. 156). Neither mere imagined doubt nor mere psychological doubt, however, is cognitively grounded doubt and hence neither yields an actual, grounded defeater of the kind sought by Nagel and Williams. In sum, then, they do not supply a compelling case against the value or the meaning of lasting human life. Instead, they leave us with an obviously bad modal inference. An endorsement, then, of the value of lasting human life with God finds no real threat here.

POWER AGAINST FLUX

Is power available to us humans that can counter any disintegrating and ultimately destructive flux in a way that secures our survival as persons who flourish? The question is big, of course, but the power in question would enable us to have a continuous life of flourishing as opposed to destruction in final death. Even so, we should not portray continuous life as immutable or even unchanging, because one's continuing to survive does not require one's being either immutable or unchanging. Our question divides into two issues. First, is there such anti-flux power available just from our own resources, that is, under our own control directly or indirectly? Second, is there such power available from a source beyond our own (human) resources, that is, from a source not under our control? The first issue attracts our attention in this section.

My own individual power, whatever value it has, fails to reverse and even to stop the onslaught of physical and personal decay surrounding and threatening us. The same is evidently true of the individual power of the other humans alive among us. As a result, it is doubtful that any individual human has the power needed to sustain our survival, let alone our flourishing survival, in the face of the surrounding deterioration and destruction. Some humans emerge at times with bold claims to special life-sustaining powers, often at a high price for others, but their true limitations surface before long, and the destruction around us continues apace. This pessimism about individual human power is eminently testable: an individual human need only try to stop the surrounding destruction. The failure of this effort will be painfully transparent, with little or no delay. Accordingly, modesty regarding an individual human's power against deterioration is clearly advisable, despite the excesses of the self-help therapy market.

Lacking needed power against the disintegrating flux, I naturally focus on, grasp, or latch onto something as an intended source of security – at least for myself, if not for others too. Let's call this an intended *stabilizer* in the flux. Something can be an intended stabilizer either for my lasting survival or, more modestly, for my current life just for a time. We also can talk about an intended stabilizer for *flourishing* survival for a person, that is, for survival that is genuinely good, or worthwhile, in a sense to be specified.

An intended stabilizer for my (or our) *lasting* flourishing survival offers a supposed means of secure flourishing survival for me (or us) without end. It therefore offers a basis for hope in a lasting future of flourishing for a person (or a group of persons). Perhaps God could provide a lasting stabilizer for us, even for flourishing survival, in virtue of divine power that gives life and resists death. "Perhaps" is the key term, however, because we have not answered the crucial question of whether God actually exists. Affirming such power without corresponding evidence for its reality would gain us little if anything. Indeed, it would amount to cheating.

An intended stabilizer for my (or our) current life *just for a time* offers a supposed means of temporary constancy or security for me (or us) that staves off death for a time. Perhaps resources from health, wealth, intelligence, and human friendship could figure in such a relatively modest stabilizer for a person. Clearly, however, a stabilizer for lasting survival would be more surprising and impressive than a stabilizer that offers just temporary security. Accordingly, we shall be concerned mainly about the availability of a stabilizer for our lasting survival, particularly for such survival that includes our lasting flourishing. Without such a stabilizer, our lives eventually will lose their goodness if not their existence as well. Mere lasting survival may be amazing, but it does not give us what we genuinely need as persons in search of what is best for us: namely, *flourishing* lasting survival, where a flourishing life is a good, worthwhile life of a sort to be specified.

For any stabilizer available to us in the flux, we will need to appropriate it in a manner that yields stabilizing in our actual experience, as required by genuine human flourishing. This appropriating will need to be under our control, if we are to be responsible for it. Do we have the control or autonomy needed in the flux to embrace a stabilizer effectively or responsibly, if one is actually available?

We might understand "autonomy" in either of two senses. The first sense involves self-sufficiency; in particular, I have autonomy in the flux if and only if I am self-sufficient with regard to my embracing a stabilizer in the flux. Given autonomy in this sense, I have the power of my own to embrace a stabilizer on my own, without any needed external power. The second sense is more modest; it requires just my capability to decide to embrace a stabilizer, and it allows that my actually embracing a stabilizer depends on an external power. For instance, I may need to request and to receive God's power to carry out successfully my decision to embrace a stabilizer. This would not undermine my capability to decide; instead, this would allow for my decision's requiring support for its execution from an outside power, such as God. My modest autonomy may rest

on my being capable to ask God for powerful divine help to carry
out my decisions.

The position of this book does not depend on our having autonomy as self-sufficiency; instead, it can proceed with the more modest kind of autonomy. Given modest autonomy, what do I or, more
importantly, *should* I pursue, serve, advance, or embrace in the flux?
One familiar answer is this: the fulfillment of my own (transitory)
desires and intentions. In that case, do I or should I pursue such
desires and intentions even against what is good for other people, in
cases of competition?

Often I latch onto something I can control, if only to try to minimize the risk of harmful severity toward myself. My having control
seems to be my safest path to my security. If something is outside
my control, I tend to regard this thing as possibly contributing to
my harm or at least as not assuredly safe for me. It might seem safe
to recommend, then, that I should pursue things under my control
that will minimize the risk of harm to me. The final story, however,
is not quite so simple, because I may need help from something or
someone not under my control if I am to have a stabilizer for my
flourishing with lasting survival. In any case, we should not disregard this option at the start. Otherwise, we could bring real harm to
ourselves in life's rigorous flux, despite our best intentions.

It is doubtful that an *a priori* philosophy, as an intellectual system
in the flux, will yield by itself a stabilizer for lasting human survival.
An effort to the contrary would be reminiscent of Plato's aforementioned redemptive strategy, but it would face a serious problem.
A philosophy, even if known *a priori*, gives no power to a person
beyond the power of the intellectual content of that philosophy and
the power of that person to accept and conform to that content.

After all, a philosophy, even if known *a priori*, is just intellectual content of a particular, philosophical kind. It is a philosophical

system of intellectual content, with more or less coherence and explanatory power, and this holds true regardless of how elaborate, sophisticated, and well grounded the philosophy is. The explanatory power of intellectual content, however, lacks the needed causal efficacy or power to underwrite lasting human survival. In addition, a philosophy, like any system of intellectual content, does not give one causal powers beyond one's ability to accept and conform to the content of that philosophy. As a result, a philosophy by itself does not significantly take one beyond an individual human's power and therefore cannot solve the problem of lasting human survival, particularly with human flourishing.

A philosophy, understood as an intellectual system, can have content or terms that refer to things beyond the parts of the intellectual system – such as events and objects. This is important, because the referents in question can have causal powers that exceed the powers of an individual human. For instance, a philosophy can include the term "God" to refer to, or denote, a God who transcends not only an intellectual system but also the power of any human. In that case, however, God would not be, strictly speaking, *part* of the relevant philosophy as an intellectual system, even though some part of the system would denote God (say, with the referring term "God"). It would be a serious confusion of intellectual content with objective referents of such content to suggest otherwise. Accordingly, any power available to humans from a transcendent God (as a referent of a term in a philosophy) would not be reducible to the power of a philosophy as a system of intellectual content. As a result, we should not confuse the redemptive power or adequacy of a philosophy with the redemptive power or adequacy of *the objects denoted* by some terms of a philosophy.

Even if each individual human lacks the power to sustain lasting survival for humans, including for himself or herself individually, we should consider the presence of other people in the flux. More specifically, we should ask this: can we save ourselves from destruction as a group, with *shared* human power that exceeds an individual human's power? Is there *social* human power that will do the needed redemptive work for us and overcome life's harmful severity? In any case, if groups of humans fail to supply the needed power, then a philosophy offered by groups of humans also will fail in this regard, for the sorts of reasons indicated previously.

Groups of humans have shown remarkable power throughout human history in a wide range of areas, including education, health, finance, sports, politics, warfare, construction, farming, and gardening. This power has far exceeded the power of any single human, and it is not reducible to any philosophy or other system of intellectual content. Even so, social human power now appears to face serious limits regarding the provision of lasting human survival with flourishing. Such power seems definitely inadequate, at least for now, to overcome death and to provide lasting and flourishing survival for all willing humans. The future may differ from the past in this regard and surprise us pleasantly, say, with startling advances in cell biology and genetic engineering that counter human aging and dying. No one should deny this as a possibility, although possibility need not match the actual world (and we need flourishing life in addition to lasting life). Imagined possibilities can be and often are shattered by the real world in its harmful severity.

Perhaps the problem of flux will yield if we move from concerns about the survival of human individuals to concerns about a solution at a generic level. Accordingly, one might propose that we focus not on individual human persons but rather on either the *species* of humans or the reality of human *personhood* (or *humanity*) as such. In that case, we would look for a stabilizer for either the human species or human personhood. Lasting life then would involve the relinquishing of individual human personal existence for the sake of the survival of something more generic.

The proposal at hand does not solve the problem of the fate of individual human persons in the grip of destructive flux. Instead, it redirects our attention to something else, to a concern about something more generic. As long as we regard individual human persons as a locus of value, we will be unsatisfied by such a proposal. We still will inquire about the fate of individual human persons, in accordance with the widely shared view that individual human persons have value. As a result, our current inquiry about human persons and flux is to the point, at least for many people. If some people want to change the subject, for something more generic, they are doing just that: changing the subject.

What exactly is involved in the relevant talk of lasting survival for humans? Does the survival in question involve just the continuation of human lives? Such mere survival is of relatively modest interest, because it would fall short of human flourishing that entails a genuinely good life. Human lives could endure indefinitely but lack the power to flourish with such goods as peace, hope, and unselfish love as alternatives to such evils as war, despair, and selfishness. We shall inquire about the genuine unselfish and righteous love called *agapē* in the Greek New Testament, because it arguably is a key to human flourishing of an important kind. In this connection, we shall ask whether lasting human flourishing can proceed with a certain amount of selfishness and therefore without *agapē* throughout.

As portrayed in the New Testament, *agapē* is one's noncoercively willing (at least when the opportunity arises) what is good rather than bad for all concerned, including one's enemies, without treating oneself as more deserving than others of good treatment. As Emil Brunner observes: "The [one] who loves with *agapē* goes also 'the second mile,' he requites evil with good, he 'turns the other cheek,' he loves his enemy (Matt. 5:39–45)" (1962, p. 310). Given the pervasiveness of human selfishness, we should ask whether such unselfish love stems from human power by itself, self-sufficiently. Accordingly, we should ask whether instead humans must receive *agapē* from a source beyond themselves if *agapē* is needed for their continued flourishing. If they must receive it thus, we should ask from whom or what they must receive it. These are pressing questions now, despite their typical neglect by philosophers.

We have considerable evidence to doubt that genuine *agapē* is solely at the discretion of human power, as if a human could exercise unselfish love, including enemy-love, always at will, self-sufficiently. Whether we acknowledge the relevant evidence may depend on how honest we are willing to be about ourselves regarding our attitudes toward other people, including our enemies. Some of the evidence comes from certain cases where people believe that loving their enemies is their best option, all things considered, but they nonetheless fail to love their enemies, even if they have a general desire to love all other people. In such cases, people may suffer *akrasia* about *agapē* toward their enemies, because their wills have not conformed to their beliefs regarding what is best, all things considered.

Cases of *akrasia* are not necessarily cases where people lack the power to follow their beliefs regarding what is best. Instead, their wills sometimes *do not* conform to their beliefs regarding what is best all things considered, but it does not follow that they *cannot* conform to these beliefs owing to a lack of power on their part. Even so, at least some cases of people failing to love their enemies (despite their believing that all of us should love our enemies) arguably involve their lack of power to love their enemies always at will, self-sufficiently.

We are hard put to identify a single mere human who plausibly can claim to love his or her enemies always at will, self-sufficiently, without qualification or exception, and this limitation is instructive now. Even if the apostle Paul, Francis of Assisi, and Mother Teresa are good candidates in the opinions of some people, these three would disown unhesitatingly the proposed exalted status regarding enemy-love, particularly as a matter of self-sufficiency. They would attribute any power of enemy-love within themselves not to their own resources but rather to the independent power of God, that is, to divine *agapē*, and the same is true of other morally exemplary figures in the Christian tradition. (I also would add the Jewish tradition, but we need not digress.) In contrast, we easily can find evidence of human hate toward one's enemies and, less extremely, of human failure to love others unselfishly. Indeed, such evidence seems pervasive among humans and even familiar in the popular media, where wide-ranging moral challenges are rarely developed by journalists. Accordingly, as Alan Richardson notes, "in the New Testament, *agapē* is not a natural virtue which men can develop within themselves if they try hard enough" (1958, p. 259).

Given that one's *agapē* should apply to one's enemies as well as one's friends, and humans very rarely love their enemies, we plausibly can doubt that humans manifest *agapē* self-sufficiently. If, by way of objection, one proposes the reality of self-sufficient *agapē* toward one's friends, then we should note that such *agapē* would be genuine only if it persisted in cases where one's friends somehow become one's vicious enemies. In other words, genuine *agapē* cannot be based on the consideration that a recipient is one's friend rather than one's enemy or even is deserving of *agapē*. Selfish friendship is not *agapē*.

Agapē is not a function of the perceived fittingness or worthiness of its objects. Instead, genuine *agapē* applies even in cases where its intended recipients do not merit or deserve *agapē*. These considerations undermine a case for the human self-sufficiency of *agapē* in situations where one appears to love one's useful friends on one's own power. In addition, the common phenomenon of one's treating oneself as more deserving of good treatment than others, at least one's enemies if not one's friends too, heightens the challenge to any such case. Regarding that familiar phenomenon, something other than genuine *agapē* is present. Clearly, not all familiar talk of "love" is talk of *agapē*. In addition, if someone claims to have the self-sufficient power of *agapē* while simply choosing not to exercise it always, then this would be a failure of *agapē* at the level of execution or practice. We naturally could question whether the self-sufficient power is actually present in such a case.

If lasting human flourishing depends on lasting divine power as its ultimate source, we can raise doubt about an approved place for selfishness in such flourishing. Regardless of whether God exists, the title "God," as used in various monotheistic traditions, demands worthiness of worship, and such worthiness requires moral perfection of the titleholder, as Chapter 1 indicated. Worthiness of worship demands worthiness of full, unqualified commitment, because worship requires full, unqualified commitment. In addition, one will be worthy of full, unqualified commitment only if one is morally without defect, that is, morally perfect.

Moral defectiveness, such as selfishness, undermines worthiness of full commitment and therefore worthiness of worship. As a result, God's character, given the title "God," must be free of selfishness and characterized instead by unselfish love, that is, *agapē*. To the extent, then, that we are selfish, to that extent we will be at odds with God's character and thus out of cooperative companionship with the source of lasting human flourishing, if God exists. To the same extent, we will not be at peace with God and hence not flourishing relative to the source of lasting human flourishing. As a result, lasting human flourishing, *if* there is such, leaves no room for human selfishness and instead demands *agapē*.

A human's need to receive *agapē* from an outside source does not entail that he or she is morally innocent or faultless for failing to love others (including enemies) unselfishly, on the ground that "ought" implies "can." One could have the power to *receive agapē* from an outside source (say, by asking the source for such outside help), even if one lacked the power on one's own, or self-sufficiently, to love unselfishly. Accordingly, we should distinguish between (a) one's lacking the power of one's own to produce *agapē*, directly or indirectly, and (b) one's lacking *available* power outside oneself that one can receive to reproduce *agapē*.

In rejecting human self-sufficiency regarding *agapē*, we can affirm the aforementioned option (a) but reject option (b). The affirmation of (a), in other words, does not entail despair about the *available human reception* of *agapē* from an independent source of power. It allows that humans can receive and reproduce *agapē* dependently, owing to their dependence on the available power of an outside source of human *agapē*. Such an outside source could support or empower (without coercing) a human choice for or against human *transformation* toward the manifestation of *agapē*. This *agapē* transformation could require one's identification with others in their suffering for their benefit, and it could be diachronic in requiring one's character formation in ever-deepening *agapē* over time, through flux, even in life's harmful severity. (Chapter 4 returns to this topic.)

INTENTIONS WITHIN FLUX

Why are we humans in this frustrating and puzzling flux of our world? This question seems important, but it might suffer from begging a key question: namely, the question of whether there actually is an explanation, purposive or nonpurposive, of our being in this flux. A better formulation is this: what, *if anything*, is behind all of the world's changes, including the movements in my experiences, such as the experienced ups and downs, comings and goings, and dyings and risings?

The fact of the world's changes seems undeniable, at least from where I sit (for a time). Is there, however, something behind it all, not just as a cause, but as a meaning-conferring explanation? In particular, is there a unifying power with constant *intentions* or *purposes* behind all of the movement or at least much of it? In other words, is there an intentional *agent* thus involved in the mix as a superhuman guide? The very idea repels many philosophers and scientists of a materialist persuasion, but this recent trend should not deter us without scrutiny. Trends come and go in philosophy and even in the sciences, for better or worse.

Perhaps the flux in question is ultimately an unexplained fluke, surrounded by futility without any ultimate explanation. Perhaps, then, there is no ultimate point or purpose to the flux, any appearances to the contrary notwithstanding. In any case, for most of the flux in what I experience, I myself do not seem to be its source; instead, it seems to be given to me or at least somehow imposed on me. Is it, however, given or imposed by an agent, that is, by an intentional agent who is superhuman? Is there, accordingly, intentional or purposive unity hidden somewhere in the flux? If so, is the flux given for good or bad, or for both? However difficult, such questions are prompted, if unintentionally, by the flux under consideration.

We may formulate our question as follows: does the flux present us with a challenge ultimately from blind *nonpurposive* forces and thus ultimately with a destructive challenge (as Bertrand Russell [1903] and many others have proposed)? Or, alternatively, is there a superhuman agent who offers a redemptive challenge in the flux, a challenge that can deliver survival with lasting flourishing for us despite the flux? Are there any indicators in the flux that favor one of these two alternatives over the other? If so, we do well to ask about the reliability of these indicators. Some progress on this front may enable us to discern whether the flux leaves us, unfortunately, with ultimate futility, with no hope of lasting human flourishing.

For better or worse, we sometimes face challenges from other human agents in the flux. Indeed, some of these challenges from humans escalate to the point of the painfully obvious, such as in cases of outright assault or warfare among humans. Do human-to-human challenges exhaust our person-to-person challenges in the flux, with no intrusion of a superhuman intentional agent? Many people assume so, especially if they are materialists, but in that case our intentional challenges and responses will be only as strong as the humans involved, even if we arguably need something stronger.

If all intentions and intentional agents in the flux are temporary in their survival, then they will be unable to sustain *lasting* human flourishing. An obvious problem in this case is that at some point they will not be around at all to sustain human flourishing; that is, they are not lasting stabilizers. At least we have no good ground to suppose that lasting human flourishing will emerge from temporary sources of flourishing. As a result, many people (following Russell) disavow hope for lasting human flourishing, even if they acknowledge the reality of some temporary human flourishing. They thus lower the bar for reliable human hope.

We experience various kinds of human power in the flux, including some from individual humans and some from groups of humans. The use of such human power is typically intentional, given that it is characteristically *aimed at a goal*, even if unreflectively. It is doubtful, however, that human power yields a full explanation of the origin of the world's flux, if only because the flux antedated the origin of humans. We can imagine that the intentional, goal-directed power in the flux exceeds human power and offers superhuman power, but imagined power is not necessarily real power. Imagination and reality sometimes move in opposing directions, as the aforementioned shattering of imagined possibilities by reality reveals.

An intentional explanation of the flux will offer an explanation in terms of the intentions of an agent or a group of agents. It therefore will not leave the flux as a complete fluke, without any explanation. A superhuman intentional explanation of the flux will offer an explanation in terms of the intentions of a superhuman agent or a group of superhuman agents. Does the flux call for any such seemingly far-fetched explanation? The quick and easy answer would be no, but we need to pursue the question carefully regarding the prospect of divine superhuman power at work in the flux. In doing so, we will give a fair hearing to a proposal of lasting human flourishing that depends on God, particularly on the power of divine *agapē*.

GOD AND FLUX

Is there divine power at work in the flux? If so, what does it look, sound, or feel like? God may be invisible, but an invisible God need not have invisible power. Many people assume that any divine power exercised toward humans would entail successful divine *control* over those humans. Such an assumption, however, does not fit with God's powerfully allowing for and even sustaining human agents who *freely* exercise their power either for or against God. We should acknowledge at least the prospect of such noncoercive divine power toward humans in the flux, however we understand the details of human freedom (for some options, see Kane 2005). This would amount to divine power that does not entail divine control over all human decisions or actions. Suppose that, motivated by perfectly unselfish *agapē*, God noncoercively seeks to have humans freely receive divine *agapē* and thereby freely exercise *agapē* toward all people in dependence on divine *agapē*. In that case, any kind of divine control that entails the coercion of all human decisions or actions would be out of place as contrary to divine intent.

We can illuminate the kind of divine power in question by specifying what its main goals would be, that is, what it would mainly aim to achieve, at least with regard to humans. One particularly noteworthy goal of divine *agapē* would be noncoerced human companionship, or cooperative fellowship, with the God who is worthy of worship and who therefore loves all humans perfectly, including humans who are enemies of God. (As Chapter 1 suggested, we may use the term "God" as a maximally honorific title – rather than a name – connoting such distinctive features.) Such companionship would require of humans noncoerced volitional cooperation with God, at least as a general intentional commitment. In other words, it would require a human to intend reverently to conform to, or obey, God's morally perfect will. A human in companionship with God could fail to obey God on occasion and therefore fall short of moral perfection, but this human's general intentional commitment to obey God would have to be in place for there to be volitional companionship with God.

A divine sustainer of human agency would seek noncoercively to transform humans, individually and collectively, from the inside out toward God's moral character, including toward perfect *agapē* for all other agents. As a result, God would intend this world's rigorous flux to be a remedial school of character formation for humans as they depend on divine noncoercive efforts to that end. This divine redemptive school would be a place of rigorous human challenge and struggle, because selfish human ways, being deep-seated and stubborn, do not yield easily to the unselfish ways of divine *agapē*. The latter consideration regarding selfishness enjoys abundant, even conclusive empirical confirmation from human behavior. (See any reliable biography or news outlet regarding human life for the confirming details.)

Our best anthropological evidence suggests that human moral self-sufficiency does not, and will not, meet a standard of unselfish divine *agapē*. Such moral self-sufficiency will fail on this front, given human moral weakness relative to the rigorous unselfishness, even toward enemies, demanded by the divine standard of *agapē*. Arguably, then, the needed human struggle is a struggle both *against* human moral self-sufficiency and *for* human dependence on divine *agapē* for the sake of receiving and manifesting unselfish *agapē* for all concerned, even one's enemies. Let's call this *the agapē struggle*. The prospect of this struggle merits careful attention, given the consistent moral failure of humans to love others unselfishly, including their enemies, in this world's rigorous flux.

The divine remedial school under consideration offers a struggle for humans to receive and manifest divine *agapē*. It also offers a struggle for humans to discern God's presence and will in the world's flux for the sake of human cooperative dependence on God's power. The relevant *agapē* struggle, accordingly, might be characterized broadly as having a cognitive component as well as moral and spiritual components. If a person is unable to discern God's presence in the flux, that person, quite naturally, will not be inclined to struggle to depend on God's *agapē*. In any case, there is a lot of distracting noise in the flux, and it is not obvious to all observers that the noise is accompanied by the presence of God. The surrounding noise calls for some interpretation or explanation, at least at first listening, and we do well to be aware of what guides and grounds our interpretation or explanation of this noise.

Our personal expectations for the surrounding flux can have a formative, and even misleading, influence on our interpretation and explanation of the flux. In particular, what we expect regarding the kinds of power available in the flux can hinder us from apprehending indicators of certain kinds of power in the flux. For instance, if I am an eliminative materialist (in the tradition of Quine 1957) who disavows the reality of intentional agents and expects only physical causes, I will not be looking for the interventions of a nonphysical intentional agent in the flux. In that case, I would be inclined to interpret any indicator of the reality of a nonphysical intentional agent as something that actually does not involve such an intentional agent. As a result, my eliminative materialist expectations would cloud relevant evidence for me in a case where I am presented with an indicator of the power of a nonphysical intentional agent at work in the flux. Ideas and expectations matter, in bad and good ways.

Many people do not expect to face a struggle on the moral and cognitive fronts to appropriate a divine intervention in human experience. Instead, they assume that if divine *agapē* were available to us humans, we would have an easy and obvious opportunity to receive it. In assuming this, however, people misunderstand or at least distort what would be the character and purposes of a God who is worthy of worship and is therefore morally perfect. Such a God would seek to redeem creation by subjecting to futility all of the obstacles to divine redemption, including all of the counterfeit gods and the unreliable stabilizers for flourishing that are embraced by humans. In other words, God would aim for some pollution control.

The idea of God's "subjecting to futility" whatever needs such subjecting for divine redemptive purposes is captured by the apostle Paul in a widely neglected but illuminating remark (as represented in Chapter 1): "The creation was subjected to futility, not by its own will, but by the One subjecting it, in hope, because the creation itself will be freed from the slavery of corruption into the freedom of the glory of the children of God" (Rom. 8:20–21, my translation). According to Paul, God subjects the creation to futility in the hope of setting people free from their bondage in corruption and thereby enabling them to enter freely into the glory of being the genuine children of God. To that hoped-for redemptive end, God shakes up, challenges, and undermines, even severely, the security pursued by humans in various sectors of creation, including in their presumed self-sufficiency apart from God. Paul finds old-fashioned idolatry at work in that human quest (on which see Rom. 1:21–25; cf. Meadors 2006).

God seeks to expose the ultimate futility of human reliance on things other than God for life's true security and flourishing, such things as wealth, health, education, fame, selfish ambition, self-serving religion, exclusive family relations, earthly longevity, and worldly power. God offers the instability of life's flux, then, as a means of preventing us from latching on to securities inadequate to sustain a flourishing life that lasts. Our presumed moral self-sufficiency, for instance, needs to give way to the realization that we belong to someone else, namely God, who alone can empower genuine *agapē* and lasting flourishing in us and among us. Is this a plausible position, in the end? One's answer will depend in part on the range of one's experience, including what is present to one in experience. This claim needs some elaboration.

PARTICIPATION IN STRUGGLE

If God is indeed present somehow in the world's flux, for the redemptive purpose suggested, then a simple but important auto-biographical question emerges: am *I* present for God's redemptive presence? That is, am I genuinely available to struggle to receive and then to manifest God's purportedly transformative *agapē*? Or, alternatively, am I preoccupied with other priorities that omit divine *agapē* and a struggle for it as a priority in my life? More concretely, if God's presence involves a kind of powerful *agapē* that includes an authoritative call to receive and obey God amidst the noise of the flux, am I willing to be adequately attentive to listen for and receive this call? In particular, is my conscience sufficiently sensitive and receptive to this life-giving call, particularly its offer and demand of unselfish *agapē*, in such a way that it enables me to hear and obey God's morally profound call? (On a divine call and the combination of offer/gift and demand regarding divine *agapē*, see Brunner 1937, pp. 114–131, 198–207; 1950, pp. 183–199.)

If I am sincerely receptive to the divine call in question, I will be available to join the *agapē* struggle in a way that resists priorities contrary to this divinely commanded struggle. To join this struggle is to join God's own life of ongoing struggle for self-giving love for all agents. Arguably, Jesus had this kind of divine expectation in mind with his austere remark that "there is need of only one thing" (Luke 10:42). His remark may seem narrow, but at the same time it may capture the heart of divine redemption for humans.

Of course, we gain nothing by begging the question about God's existence in the flux of life. Mere belief that God exists will yield no lasting antidote to the destructive flux. Instead, the present recommendation is to be both sincerely open to a subtle divine invitation to *agapē* struggle in the flux and genuinely attentive to any indicators of divine involvement for the sake of such struggle. A way of testing the redemptive theism in question is to accept that recommendation with honesty and then to assess one's subsequent experience accordingly over time. In this case, God ultimately must deliver the needed experiential and evidential goods at the suitable time for each receptive person. If the best available explanation of one's experience supports such theism, then one can move beyond fideism and question begging to (affirmation of) well-grounded belief in God (see Moser 2010a, chaps. 2, 4; cf. Wiebe 2004, chap. 5). Given that God's character of *agapē* is not purely conceptual, the needed evidential support for humans must have a basis in human experience. (Chapter 3 returns to the topic of evidence and experience of God.)

The previous considerations raise the issue of how we might remove obstacles between God and us, in order to participate in God's powerful life of *agapē* for others, including God's redemptive suffering for the world. Those considerations also prompt the question of whether God's suffering for the world, such as in the self-giving death of Jesus Christ for others (see Rom. 5:8; cf. Moser 2008, chap. 3; 2010a, chap. 4), aims to do something other than to preserve or secure the world *as it is*. The question is whether the aim instead is to redeem the world in a new mode of life in cooperation with God, where *agapē* for others, including enemy-love, is the norm and the operative power for all receptive agents. We are now on conceptual soil foreign to traditional philosophy, as we should expect in the presence of a challenging God worthy of worship. (On the latter point, see 1 Cor. 1:18–25; cf. Hays 1997, chap. 1, Gorman 2001, pp. 275–280.)

The primary concern of a truly redemptive God would be not so much with the specific intellectual content embraced by humans as with their willingly joining an *agapē*-deepening struggle for others, in dependence on the God who is the source of perfect *agapē* for humans. This struggle would be as much a struggle (in cooperation) *with* God as a struggle *for* (the redemptive mission of) God. In the divine remedial school, God would struggle with humans for the sake of their *agapē*-oriented transformation, both when they resist (at least without final rejection) and when they cooperate (if imperfectly). In other words, God would participate in the *agapē* struggle for the sake of disseminating and deepening the noncoercive power of divine *agapē* among humans. To that end, God would engage in self-giving suffering for the benefit of humans, as important parts of Jewish and Christian theology suggest (on which see Heschel 1962, Fiddes 1988).

Given *agapē*-focused redemptive purposes for humans, God would aim to have us be in a distinctive relation to truth, in order to accommodate the *reality* of the purported redemption anchored in divine *agapē*. The aim would be not just that we know that particular claims are true but, more importantly, that we ourselves become true to (that is, in full agreement with) divine *agapē*, because the intended redemption in *agapē* is for *us ourselves*, and not just for our beliefs. Kierkegaard puts the point as follows: "Christianly understood, truth is obviously not [just] to know the truth but to be the truth … [O]nly then do I in truth know the truth, when it becomes a life in me" (1850, pp. 205–206; cf. Moser and McCreary 2010). Accordingly, the reality of divine *agapē* must become a powerful life, not just an object of reflection, in us. Divine severity can serve that redemptive end in pointing to needed priorities for humans, as long as humans cooperate.

The suggested incarnational approach to redemptive truth goes beyond any merely intellectual relation to truth. It requires that the reality of divine *agapē* become the motivational center of our lives in order to have us become personally reflecting, or imaging, of God's moral character, ever more deeply. This incarnational relation is *personifying* toward redemptive truth, and not merely intellectual, because divine *agapē* exceeds intellectual matters and involves a human *as a personal, intentional agent* with a life to live resolutely in the face of severity. More specifically, the purported redemption in *agapē* involves agreeably received, cooperative personal transformation toward God's moral character, and not just new knowledge, in virtue of a person's willingly receiving and manifesting divine *agapē* for all persons, even one's enemies.

The incarnational approach portrays God as coming to humans by judging, or subjecting to futility, all that is anti-God. The divine aim is to make willing humans new in the moral image and the companionship of the God who puts *agapē* first, even toward enemies. This redemptive judgment works via willing human appropriation of redemptive truth whereby one struggles to participate in God's moral character and life, including in the power of divine unselfish *agapē*. The litmus test for the divine authenticity of this struggle available to humans is the *experienced realization* of the aforementioned *agapē* struggle, including a struggle for enemy-love. In the absence of a struggle for enemy-love, in particular, one is not engaged in a struggle for or with the God worthy of worship. Accordingly, much of what goes under the category of "religion" does not positively involve the God worthy of worship. Much of it is, in fact, counterfeit and anti-God, despite any appearance or language of piety. (For examples, see Juergensmeyer 2003, Stern 2003; cf. Seibert 2009).

When one is willing, the *agapē* struggle in the flux takes one beyond mere wishful thinking about God to the transformation of humans in volitional companionship with God. This struggle involves a meeting with God that includes an invitation and a demand: an invitation to cooperative life with God and a demand to be conformed to God's moral character of unselfish *agapē*. Some people acknowledge a call to such a divine–human meeting; others do not. The resulting disagreement is familiar and undeniable, and it should come as no surprise on reflection.

The failure of some humans to acknowledge God's presence in the *agapē* struggle arises from various sources; as a result, we have no simple explanation on this front. Many different voices populate the flux of this world, and the remarkable multiplicity leaves many people confused and doubtful. The cacophony leaves them not knowing what the needed redemptive gift of God would sound or look like. In addition, many people opt for selfishness and for hate of enemies over genuine *agapē*, and this choice creates a bias against acknowledgment of a God committed to *agapē* toward all agents.

Some people announce their desire not to be in a world governed by God, owing to fear of losing their autonomy (see Nagel 1997, p. 130). We should distinguish, however, between autonomy as independence of God and autonomy as capability to choose for or against a life of *agapē*. The latter autonomy is genuinely good and would be preserved by a God worthy of worship, but the former autonomy is arguably not good at all, given that humans lack the power to sustain their lasting flourishing on their own. If humans need to depend on God for their lasting flourishing, then their independence of God will bring trouble in its wake.

We must pay careful attention to the whole range of our experience in the flux, because the indication of God's reality should be expected to be subtle and even elusive. We should not expect divine revelation to be cheap and easy, given its unsurpassed value and profundity and our deep need for transformation toward divine *agapē*. A key issue is whether we can find self-giving suffering love at work in the flux, because divine *agapē* toward wayward humans would be inherently marked by such love. This would be intentional *agapē* for the sake of others, grounded in one's looking to practice *agapē* for the good of others even when severity and suffering come to oneself. If we find such redemptive *agapē* manifested by God, we should consider whether it can serve as a potential constant or stabilizer in the flux, even if humans must struggle to receive it and to manifest it for others.

What ultimately matters for the divine redemption of humans is *God's power* of *agapē*, not any human philosophy, metaphysics, cosmology, epistemology, hermeneutics, morality, theology, or other kind of human theory. We have considered the view, widely neglected among philosophers and others, that God's redemptive power is available to humans in the struggle of obedient receptivity toward the offer and demand of unselfish *agapē*, and not in mere thinking, talking, theorizing, or even arguing. This is *dynamic, Gethsemane theism*, because it identifies God's redemptive power and corresponding self-revelation and evidence in connection with a salient challenge that calls for the struggle of human receptivity and activity, including active obedience on the part of humans. It assumes that God's redemptive power must give us humans, without coercion, the challenge and the stability we need if we are to survive and flourish lastingly in the face of life's severity.

According to Gethsemane theism, our lasting well-being comes from someone other than a mere human, as a humanly unmerited gift given noncoercively to willing humans at God's appointed time. This gift, however, comes with judgment on the world that is anti-God, not as the condemnation of humans but as subjecting to futility all that is anti-God in order to bring flourishing to humans in companionship with God. In coming with such redemptive judgment, this divine gift must be received in the aforementioned *agapē* struggle if it is to be received at all. The redemption on offer is thus dynamic rather than static. The interaction of Gethsemane is the model.

One's being evidentially assured of God's reality and role in the *agapē* struggle is diachronic rather than once and for all, or synchronic, given that the divinely desired character transformation occurs over time, and not all at once. Even though the beginning of the struggle occurs at a particular moment, the decisive evidence in the struggle builds over time as a person struggles willingly and increasingly deeply with and for God. Accordingly, the *agapē* struggle is an interactive person-to-person relationship that develops over time. Its characteristic evidence likewise yields knowledge of God over time, contrary to a familiar philosophical norm of knowledge of God as synchronic.

We should acknowledge some *pre-receptive* evidence for God, perhaps in conscience, where a person has initial evidence for God's self-manifestation but does not cooperate with God at all. Such evidence would be elusive, unstable, and thin, because God would not want people to rest content with it, apart from cooperating with God. Consider a resolute enemy of God such as the Biblical character called "Satan," who believes that God exists but does not receive God cooperatively as the Lord of his life. Satan can reasonably believe (on elusive, pre-receptive evidence) that God exists, because God has self-manifested divine reality to Satan *to a very limited extent*. However, in rejecting God, Satan has freely prevented God from manifesting divine reality to a redemptive, cooperative extent, where God's powerful love is poured out in his heart (see Rom. 5:5). Satan is not receptive to God at all, and his pre-receptive evidence does not amount to the kind of salient transformative evidence arising from cooperation with God (on which see Chapter 3).

In conclusion, given suitable experience, we may think of this world's rigorous flux as, at least in part, God's instrument for redemption in an *agapē* struggle, even for some of the evil parts of the flux not caused by God. We cognitively limited humans do not have, and should not expect to have, a full explanation of the world's tragic and horrifying evil, but we still can have a perfectly loving sustainer with us in the rigorous flux. Paul puts the point as the fact that nothing is able to separate willing humans from the *agapē* of God, neither tribulation, distress, persecution, famine, peril, death, nor any other thing (Rom. 8:35). Such a "theodicy" of *nonseparation* from God's *agapē* is ultimately the only theodicy on offer for us humans now. Given our real cognitive limits regarding God, a quest for a full explanation of God's purposes in allowing evil is sure to fail in our current predicament.

We now can begin to understand the otherwise cryptic remark at the center of the ministry of Jesus: "*Struggle* to enter through the narrow door, because many, I tell you, will seek to enter and not be able" (Luke 13:24). Famously, Socrates remarked that the unexamined life is not worth living, but we now can add that the nonstruggling life relative to divine *agapē* is not worth living either. Religion and philosophy, then, should make room for the kind of wisdom that includes a divinely offered and commanded *agapē* struggle and its corresponding distinctive epistemology. This sca change would yield profound benefits for religion and philosophy as wisdom-oriented disciplines. The test of authenticity, ultimately, is in the living through the *agapē* struggle on offer. The next chapter turns to the distinctive epistemology in question.

CHAPTER THREE

Severity and evidence

I thank you, Father, Lord of heaven and earth, because you
have hidden these things from the wise and the intelligent and
have revealed them to infants; yes, Father, for such was your
gracious will.

(Matt. 11:25–26; Luke 10:21)

Our intellectual sophistication is nowadays so great that it is difficult to achieve, or to recover, that naked contact of our minds
with the confronting reality out of which true wisdom alone can
be born. Jesus said, "Except ye become as little children."

(Baillie 1956, p. 141)

As the Introduction suggested, many people have misguided expectations for God, that is, expectations that fail to match what would
be God's *purposes*, if God exists. Such expectations cloud human
recognition and appropriation of the evidence for God that would
be on offer. This evidence, being evidence for God, would be volitionally rigorous in a manner illustrated by the Gethsemane crisis-
experience of Jesus. This chapter develops this neglected theme.

GETHSEMANE AGAIN

The reality of severity in human life includes the reality of deep
experiential and volitional conflict in humans. In humans struggling with God, such conflict has a name and even a historical
location: *Gethsemane*. A deficiency of religious life and thought,

including in Christian and Jewish variations, is their failure to give due import to Gethsemane and its disturbing, severe God. In shunning Gethsemane and the priority of God's will, people become world-bound and thereby obscure any distinctive evidence of God in themselves and for themselves; hence the spiritual flatness among many human, even religious communities. Indeed, we humans are experts at fleeing or otherwise avoiding the needed volitional crisis of Gethsemane.

Gethsemane is no picnic garden; instead, it is a context of human struggle with the presence and the priority of God's morally perfect character and will. The best example is Jesus of Nazareth in the Judean location called "Gethsemane." Bent on obeying God, for the sake of introducing God's kingdom and thereby the priority of God's will, Jesus found himself called by God to offer his life in self-sacrifice to God for the sake of others. This was a moral struggle between Jesus and God, where Jesus anticipated his arrest and crucifixion by Roman officials as part of God's seemingly foolish plan to redeem humans. God, however, invites and nudges people toward Gethsemane; they do not have to find it on their own. We may think of this as part of God's severe prevenient grace.

Chapter 1 introduced the following portrait sketched in Mark's Gospel:

[Jesus and his disciples] went to a place called Gethsemane … He said to them, "I am deeply grieved, even to death …" [H]e threw himself on the ground and prayed that, if it were possible, the hour [of his arrest and crucifixion] might pass from him. He said, "Abba, Father, for you all things are possible; remove this cup [of suffering and death] from me; yet, not what I want, but what you want." (Mark 14:32–36)

Gethsemane, as Chapter 1 indicated, begins with a humanly experienced conflict, between a human want and a divine want, but ideally resolves in a sincere human plea to God for the realization of God's will as a priority. Accordingly, a fitting human approach to God puts God's will first, prior to merely human preferences. Perhaps humans can find the elusive God under consideration, not in mere reflection but instead in the experiential and volitional conflict of Gethsemane, where God offers to redeem and to befriend humans on God's perfect but rigorous terms.

Gethsemane is a personal context for a divine–human interaction and relationship that challenge world-bound, or anti-God, human ways. The challenge can be rigorous for humans, given long-standing bad habits at odds with divine purposes and expectations for humans. Following Jesus in Gethsemane, however, humans can begin to apprehend and to obey God *as God*, as the one with morally perfect authority over humans, including over their desires and intentions. In that context, modeling Jesus, humans should allow God's moral character, will, and reality to emerge as a priority, in the manner desired by God. They thereby would allow salient evidence to emerge for the God who, being morally perfect, merits supremacy in human struggles with God.

Let us think of a suitable Gethsemane response by a human as involving *divine corrective reciprocity*, because it includes not just a person's knowing God but God's knowing that person correctively in virtue of challenging that person in conscience and being cooperatively received (and perhaps even consistently obeyed) *as God* by that person. We should not confuse, however, one's cooperatively receiving God and one's consistently obeying God; the latter often requires a long struggle of maturity in companionship with God.

We should distinguish between divine corrective reciprocity and *divine corrective inquiry*. A human inquirer can find that he or she is being correctively inquired of by God as God's will emerges as a challenge in human conscience. In such inquiry, God questions one relative to one's meeting the standard of God's perfect moral character and will. This kind of inquiry can occur in various specific ways, with various particular challenges. We limited humans cannot complete the list of ways in which God can bring corrective inquiry to humans. The common feature, however, is God's challenging one sincerely to acknowledge one's falling short of God's perfect standard and therefore needing divine redemption. This is a challenge to embrace cooperative dependence on God and to relinquish human self-sufficiency before God. It is a divine attempt to have humans become reconciled to God, cooperatively and noncoercively, for the sake of lasting human life with God.

Divine corrective inquiry can be a salient feature of human experience, including human conscience, and it can occur over time, if not at a moment. This kind of religious experience of God is widely neglected by philosophers and others, but it fits well with the redemptive moral character of a God worthy of worship. We should not regard the divine corrective inquiry in question as coercive. Humans can ignore or repress it as they resolve not to make God's will a priority in their lives. As a result, divine corrective inquiry can fall short of successful correction in divine corrective reciprocity; only the latter reciprocity requires God's being received as God by a person. Divine corrective reciprocity, going beyond mere divine inquiry, would consist in *mutual* receptivity in a divine–human interaction, where God's receptive invitation of *agapē* strikes first, always prior to any human response. Human receptivity toward God, in others words, is always a willing, agreeable response to God's prior invitation to human reconciliation in divine *agapē*.

James S. Stewart has pointed in the direction of divine corrective inquiry with his important notion of *the divine self-verification of Christ in conscience*:

This is a very wonderful thing which happens: you begin exploring the fact of Christ, perhaps merely intellectually and theologically – and before you know where you are, the fact is exploring *you*, spiritually and morally … You set out to see what you can find in Christ, and sooner or later God in Christ finds you. That is the self-verification of Jesus. (1940, pp. 87–88; cf. Mackintosh 1912, p. 319; Richardson 1966, p. 105)

Many people testify to their having a religious experience of this kind, but philosophers and theologians have neglected it widely. In doing so, they have neglected important and distinctive evidence for the reality of God in Christ. This book aims to counter this neglect (particularly in the discussion following immediately and in Chapter 5).

The characteristic broad sequence for Gethsemane, as it bears on evidence for God from divine corrective inquiry, is this: (a) God somehow prompts a human to inquire of God directly or indirectly; (b) this human then inquires of God, perhaps only about God's existence; (c) God intervenes in this person's experience with a challenging manifestation from God's perfect character and will; and (d) this person is left with a challenge to internalize and cooperate with God's will as a priority rather than to neglect it. The inquiring human, accordingly, becomes inquired of by God in virtue of a manifestation and challenge from God. The human questioner becomes the one being questioned by God, perhaps by a salient challenge in conscience. This is the experiential heart of divine corrective inquiry, and humans, as voluntary agents, can repress it to their demise.

Humans can resist divine correction in experience for any number of anti-God motives. Human selfishness, pride, and despair loom large in the familiar list, but they do not exhaust the list. Human diversion and superficiality also figure in any such list, as Pascal made clear. Gethsemane is where humans should allow

God's corrective moral *power* to be apprehended and internalized for what it is: *divine* (and hence authoritative) rather than human. In that case, humans would properly receive God's moral power (to some extent), and God's intervention would move from divine corrective inquiry to divine corrective reciprocity. In the development of such reciprocity, humans not only welcome but also *become* salient evidence of God's moral character and reality as they conform to this moral character. Humans thus would participate in and manifest God's corrective moral character. God then would be humanly personified, if imperfectly, but still remain the God who is irreducible to humans.

Albert Schweitzer rightly hinted at the importance of volitional cooperation by humans with the divine will:

No personality of the past can be transported alive into the present by means of historical observation or by discursive thought about his authoritative significance. We can achieve a relation to such a personality only when we become united with him in the knowledge of a shared aspiration, when we feel our will is clarified, enriched, and enlivened by his will and when we rediscover ourselves through him … Only thus does Jesus create a fellowship amongst us. (1913, p. 486)

A Gethsemane fellowship would be anchored in the union of human volitional cooperation with the will of God in Christ.

Schweitzer adds:

[Jesus] says the same words, "Follow me!," and sets us to those tasks which he must fulfill in our time; He commands. And to those who hearken to him, … he will reveal himself in the peace, the labours, the conflicts, and the suffering that they may experience in his fellowship, … and they will learn who he is. (1913, p. 487)

The self-revelation of God, on God's terms, is central to Gethsemane, but volitional receptivity and cooperation from humans enable humans to come alive to God's corrective moral character. It takes at least two wills to cooperate in the manner required by Gethsemane. God cannot go solo here, contrary to some excessive and misleading approaches to divine sovereignty. (Chapter 5 returns to the key idea of volitional cooperation and union with God.)

Outside of a Gethsemane context, humans lack adequate parameters for receiving salient evidence of God's moral character, will, and reality. Outside such a context, we fail to apprehend at first hand the powerful evidence of God's authoritative redemptive work for us, including that through Jesus Christ as our forerunner and intentional guide in Gethsemane. Outside of Gethsemane, it is too easy to conjoin so-called evidence of God (such as supposed evidence of a First Cause or a Designer) with other evidence and end up with a false god. This is a serious, if widely overlooked, threat to much natural theology (to which this chapter returns).

The Gethsemane model of divine–human interaction is no mere moralism just about what is morally good or bad. On the contrary, it requires human responsiveness and volitional conformity *to God*, who intervenes first and aims, in corrective reciprocity, to sustain divine–human cooperation toward the redemption of humans. Faith in God, according to this model, is not a human leap in the dark; nor is it just faith in God's *existence* or mere belief that God exists. Instead, it is the cooperative human *response to God* of yielding oneself to (participating in) God's perfect moral character and will. (Chapters 4 and 5 return to this theme; see also Moser 2010a, chap. 2.)

ARCHIMEDEAN POINT

Philosophers have long looked for an Archimedean point to perceive the world aright and then act accordingly. A secret among humans is that Gethsemane is that Archimedean point whereby one can confront God directly, with due human receptivity. This is a "secret" mainly for volitional rather than intellectual reasons, because many humans are *unwilling* to go to a Gethsemane context and then experience, obediently, the powerful corrective inquiry and evidence of God's reality. We should expect, however, that God intervenes only *as God* and therefore only on the authoritative divine end of a Gethsemane interaction that is corrective but does not undermine human agency. God presents God's moral character, and this character calls for human conformity, even inwardly, to divine *agapē*.

In our selfishness and pride, we often prefer not to be on the yielding, and corrected, end toward God. *I* often prefer to advise God in Gethsemane: *My* will be done, God, *not* yours. This reverses the model of Gethsemane offered by Jesus Christ as God's representative. God, however, will not offer Godself as a pawn for humans, lest what humans need – a morally perfect redeemer and companion – be undermined or destroyed. Indeed, God's purpose behind the severity of many human circumstances is arguably to encourage us to cooperate sincerely in Gethsemane with God. This fits with the aforementioned insight from the apostle Paul:

the creation was subjected to futility, not of its own will but by the will of the one [namely, God], who subjected it in hope that the creation itself will be set free from its bondage to decay and will obtain the freedom of the glory of the children of God. (Rom. 8:21)

Such life-giving freedom is on offer in the severity of Gethsemane, in God's deep, volitional deliverance of cooperative humans from their anti-God ways.

In the tradition of Plato and Aristotle, many philosophers seek an Archimedean point via a tenable epistemology, or at least a theory of evidence. Before a God worthy of worship, however, our epistemology must be inherently *volitional* and not merely intellectual.

It must be an epistemology of Gethsemane that can accommodate divine corrective reciprocity inwardly at the level of the human will. Arguably, humans should expect to need God's direct and specific evidential help, via divine self-revelation, in their coming to know God. This fits with the position of traditional monotheism that God is *sui generis* in perfect moral character and thus without true substitutes regarding a source for firsthand evidence.

No program of human self-help, intellectual or otherwise, will deliver what a Gethsemane context can offer: God's presence and corrective challenge to humans in their receptive conscience toward God. Of course, God's presence can be mediated to some extent by a human experiencing God, but this does not undermine or exclude God's actual presence in human experience. Mediation is not exclusion. Otherwise, interpersonal interaction itself would be at risk.

On reflection, we should not expect to come to know God solely via non-God, naturalistic, or quasi-scientific premises. A severely redemptive God would play a direct, rigorous experiential and volitional role at the very beginning of firsthand evidence in an epistemology suited to Gethsemane. So, in a Gethsemane context, we would not acknowledge God *just* in the conclusion of a merely propositional argument; otherwise, we would omit a crucial *de re* factor regarding God's intervening moral character. Similarly, we should not presume to be able to *think* or *reason* our way into God's presence or approval. Instead, aiming for redemption, God in a Gethsemane context would call for our volitional resolve to accommodate God's will inwardly over time and now, diachronically as well as synchronically. Even so, we have no recipe for control over the timing of divine intervention in our lives. We humans still need to "wait on the Lord" for the suitable time of intervention favored by God, and this is no surprise, on reflection. To this extent, at least, divine self-revelation involves some mystery from the perspective of our limited human cognition.

Perhaps we should not even ask about God's rigorously profound existence if we are unwilling to undergo Gethsemane with sincerity, because we then are probably inclined to ask about a false god. We are probably interested in a god who reflects and approves our own wills rather than the perfect divine will. Judicious truth-seeking requires, however, that we be sincerely open to a redemptive God who meets us directly, person-to-person, in a Gethsemane context of our willingness to yield to God. Accordingly, we should be open to God's wanting to be known by us in the second person, in an I–Thou Gethsemane relationship, and not merely in the third person, as he, she, or it.

After all, a truly redemptive God would seek to have humans share in the morally perfect divine character, given our need of inward moral transformation toward God's character (cf. 2 Pet. 1:3–4). For this reason, according to Abraham Heschel, "the test of [personal redemptive] truth can take place only through the soul's confrontation with God, … confronting oneself as one is confronted by God" (1973, p. 165). The center of this I–Thou confrontation is God's unique moral character and will aimed at the redemption of cooperative humans, in companionship with God.

A God worthy of worship, being morally perfect, would be a *personal*, or intentional, agent who may choose to be known by humans only via human acquaintance with God's moral character and will. This acquaintance would emerge in the conflict of a Gethsemane context, as God reveals via human conscience the divine will and the ultimate futility of life without God. Such a revelation could occur over time and need not be restricted to a moment. Only God, in any case, can show us God directly, given God's unique moral character, but we must allow for the needed time and attention to appropriate God's self-manifestation.

The divine redemption of a person involves the voluntary agency of the person being redeemed and does not extinguish that agency. Otherwise, genuine intentional agents would not be the recipients of divine redemption, and God's plan of salvation would fail. For the sake of redeeming humans, then, God would aim to show us God in a Gethsemane context, in a transformation of genuine human wills based in an I–Thou acquaintance with God.

Evidence for God must be evidence for a personal agent worthy of worship. So, not all of God's effects as creator (for instance, the purely physical world) are evidence for God. Only God's personal moral character and will can give salient evidence of an agent worthy of worship, and Gethsemane is the fitting context for apprehending this evidence. To avoid any personal challenge from God in Gethsemane, many people clamor instead for merely *de dicto* (propositional) arguments for God's existence, but God may prefer to meet people directly, in an I–Thou interaction in a redemptive Gethsemane context. God would have no cognitive need, in offering human knowledge of God, for the arguments of traditional natural theology or the abstract speculations of philosophers. This fact goes against the grain of much philosophy of religion but is confirmed by careful reflection on God's redemptive character. (This chapter returns to this controversial point.)

DIVINE AND HUMAN HIDING

We now can approach the troubling question of why God is not more obvious to everyone, if God seeks the deep deliverance of all humans. Evidently, divine hiding is sometimes too severe for us and prompts us to move toward agnosticism, atheism, or even unyielding despair about human life in general. Cognitively limited humans should not expect to have a complete explanation of the motives for divine hiding, but we can identify a key consideration in such hiding. God would want to uphold the supreme *value* of God's moral character and power, including in relation to humans, and therefore would challenge human tendencies to underestimate or trivialize this value. If *casual* human access, such as merely intellectual access, to God would diminish God's perceived value for humans, God would avoid such access. We thus might think of divine evidence as "live it or lose it" for humans, given its vital importance for humans. Correspondingly, God would be elusive in some cases for good redemptive reasons, to maintain what is good for humans who are indifferent or opposed to God. In short, God would not destroy the corrective medicine needed by humans in a Gethsemane context.

Because we are morally frail and not God, we need hopeful direction from the God who rescues willing humans. Without this direction, we have no enduring, or lasting, hope against unyielding despair, whatever our short-term hopes. We need divine direction that is not a mere suggestion or proposal for us but includes a *command* for our deep, volitional deliverance. God hides in Gethsemane with the command to let God be God, authoritative over frail human wills, and this command emerges in receptive human conscience at the fitting time. To the extent that we hide from the divine challenge of Gethsemane, God may hide from us. To the extent that we welcome God's corrective moral power in Gethsemane, we eventually receive God's salient presence and deep deliverance; that is, we receive an inwardly new life. One's personal will thus matters in apprehending evidence of God's reality, given God's purpose for the deep, volitional deliverance of humans. God is no mere entertainer of humans. Instead, God upholds God's redemptive value for humans.

Our questions about divine evidence now become personal, too personal for a merely academic setting. Maybe we need divine volitional deliverance from a *merely* academic setting. At any rate, a deeply personal question emerges: are we ourselves agreeable now to a Gethsemane context, or have we been available and willing to go there, ever, to hear, reverence, and worship God? Have we given the needed time and attention to this place of corrective personal challenge by God? If not, why not? Are we fleeing or otherwise avoiding Gethsemane, for the sake of our own short-lived will and purpose, perhaps owing to selfish fear? Arguably, many of us are, and this is the downside of the human predicament of moral pride, failure, and despair. No appeal to academic impartiality can undermine or replace the importance of such personal, inherently volitional questions involving God and humans.

We can test our answers now with a simple question: when, if ever, did we sacrifice our time to be fully available to reverence God in a Gethsemane context, if God should call us? Part of the difficulty of Gethsemane for us is its requirement that we acknowledge our own selfishness and pride and thus engage in corrective self-judgment. This is painful in a personally deep manner, and hence personal interaction with God is not cheap and easy. We rarely, if ever, set aside the time for a Gethsemane interaction, and therefore we miss out on vital evidence for God. We blithely demand salient evidence for God's presence, but we resist being *present to God*, on God's terms, in a Gethsemane context. Humans often hide from God, and then complain that God is not available to them. Something is clearly wrong with this human tendency. Perhaps God's presence is, for redemptive purposes, sensitive to our presence to God. Perhaps divine *agapē* must be cooperatively received by us as an unsurpassed priority. These are real, if neglected, options worthy of our attention.

Are we *willing* to live for the long haul in a Gethsemane context, in the obedient mode represented by Jesus Christ as our ongoing model and intentional guide for relating to God? Our actual, observable lives typically offer a definite answer, in terms of how we spend our time and respond to our tendencies toward selfishness, pride, despair, superficiality, diversion, and lack of forgiveness. We easily fall into a life mode other than a Gethsemane context, perhaps because our alternative to Gethsemane feels like a path of least resistance. Moral *resistance*, however, is exactly what we would need in the presence of a morally perfect God, lest we ourselves play or trivialize God and destroy ourselves. Hence, we should expect the severity of God in this connection, at least. We have considerable skill, not for the better, in playing or trivializing God on various fronts, given our resistance to the severe challenge of Gethsemane anchored in God's perfect moral character.

The Good News of the Christian message is that God is resolutely *for* all people (on God's perfect terms) and that all people willing to cooperate in Gethsemane will find God eventually and come to know God as God. They will find deep, volitional deliverance by God from the selfishness, pride, and despair that undermine humans and their vulnerable communities. This deliverance is a divine work in progress, and not perfected yet, in humans, but deep deliverance it is. It is a deeply experienced, lived reality for some, and no mere theory subject to merely academic assessment. We can study it *on God's terms*, but we cannot control it on human terms. It is person-engaging toward volitional cooperation with God, or it remains hidden from holdouts. For good reason, God will not be governed by familiar human ways; that is, God will not sacrifice God's goodness or destroy God's redemptive value. Otherwise, the redemption of humans would be a lost cause. The vigorous medicine we often need would no longer be available to us. Unyielding despair would emerge as a compelling option.

When the Gospel of John remarks that "the life was the light of all people" (1:4), the writer has in mind the life of Jesus Christ, including his decisive crisis of Gethsemane. His yielding in Gethsemane, as our intentional prototype and guide, made deep illumination from God *available* to all humans, but humans still must *appropriate* this illumination by following suit in a Gethsemane context, to let God be God in their lives. In other words, humans can obstruct evidence from God by putting their will ahead of God's will and thereby obscuring God's will, including its perfect goodness.

If my selfish will has first place in my life, I will be inclined to regard an unselfish will as inferior or at least practically irrelevant in comparison with my own will. In particular, I will be inclined to regard the unselfish will of God in Jesus Christ as beside the point, relative to my own selfish will. H. R. Mackintosh has characterized the person who has put his selfish will first: "He cannot see what Christ is for. He cannot believe that Christ is of any use to him. It does not dawn on him that in this man the Father is stooping down to bless and save us" (1938a, p. 119). Such a selfish will in conflict with God would obscure God's unselfish will, at least regarding its urgent goodness for all concerned. Such obscuring removes the salience from crucial evidence for God's reality and moral character.

Gethsemane supplies a practical cognitive model for humans to live by, constantly, and not just to talk about. Indeed, people should test its veracity regarding God's reality with sincere attentiveness to it and interaction with it, in order to see if divine corrective inquiry and even reciprocity emerges in their experience via conscience. Such an experiential, experimental approach fits perfectly with God's character of honesty and welcoming invitation toward humans.

A Gethsemane context counters our cheap and easy talk about God, for our own good, and opens a vital, if severe, experiential path to God. It enables humans to become awake to God's corrective interventions in human experience via God's perfect will. Given human cooperation, Gethsemane puts our priorities and our use of time in the right order, thereby bringing integrity and focus to our fragile lives before God. It takes us beyond a merely intellectual "worldview" to reverent companionship via volitional cooperation with God, an urgent need for humans. Any accompanying severity can be redeemed by God in the divine–human struggle of Gethsemane, even if we lack a full explanation of God's specific purposes.

GREATER AND LESSER MIRACLES

Salient evidence of God in a Gethsemane context includes, as we cooperate, evidence of God's deep, volitional deliverance of us from our tendencies to disobey God in our selfishness, pride, despair, and superficiality. Such evidence emerges in Paul's epistemologically important remark: "Hope [in God] does not disappoint us, because God's *agapē* has been poured into our hearts through the Holy Spirit that has been given to us" (Rom. 5:5). This is arguably the most important epistemological statement in the New Testament and in Christian literature generally, but its importance is widely neglected among philosophers and theologians. Paul would endorse a similar view about the evidential foundation of *faith*, or trust, in God. As a result, hope and faith in God are not groundless in Paul's perspective; they have a salient evidential foundation in *agapē* from God that floods a human person inwardly. Accordingly, the *agapē* in question is genuine evidence of God, and from God. This crucial lesson is widely ignored among philosophers, theologians, and others; so, correction is overdue.

Paul has in mind the *agapē* from God as the compassionate and merciful supernatural will that can be experienced by humans on

God's redemptive terms. This will, according to Paul, is exemplified perfectly in Jesus Christ, including in his response in Gethsemane, and it seeks to bring lasting good life to receptive humans, even enemies of God. (Enemies of God can become receptive, if they are willing.) Divine *agapē*, according to Paul, is the salient evidential and powerful antidote to disappointment in God, because it amounts to "God with us," but a wayward human can repress this antidote nonetheless. That is, a human can resist being in volitional cooperation with God by disregarding or rejecting the priority of God's will. A Gethsemane context offers the challenge for humans to appropriate divine *agapē* as life-forming in reverent companionship with God, in contrast with selfishness, pride, despair, superficiality, and lack of forgiveness. This *agapē* is reportedly experienced widely by humans, and it offers a distinctive experiential foundation for evidence and knowledge of God.

John Baillie remarks:

I just cannot read the Gospel story without knowing that I am being sought out in *agapē*, that I am at the same time being called to life's most sacred task and being offered life's highest prize. For it is the *agapē* God has shown me in Christ that constrains me to the love of my fellow men. If there be someone who is aware of no such constraint, I cannot of course hope to make him aware of it by speaking these few sentences. That would require, not so much a more elaborate argument as something quite different from any argument. (1963, chap. 14, with *agapē* inserted for *love*)

Arguably, the human experience of *agapē* is God's call to reconciliation and companionship in a Gethsemane context. It prompts the life-defining human crisis of deciding whether to cooperate, resist, or ignore. At any rate, the experienced power of *agapē* from God is not merely imaginary or wishful thinking; something must actually have this power to promulgate it. It is as real, and as good, as anything on offer, and this truth can be confirmed in divine corrective reciprocity, as God self-authenticates God's perfect moral character to a receptive human. Our welcoming (or neglecting) God's call is our welcoming (or neglecting) God and salient evidence of God.

No mere claim or subjective human experience is self-authenticating for God's reality (see Moser 2008, p. 149). Even so, *God* can be self-authenticating, self-attesting, or self-witnessing, in virtue of God's making God known directly to receptive humans. As an intentional agent with causal powers, God can self-manifest facts and corresponding truths regarding God. In particular, God can self-manifest to humans an *agapē*-filled moral character and will in a Gethsemane challenge. With divine corrective inquiry in human experience, the Source of humanly experienced *agapē* can self-reveal (to receptive humans) to be beyond *merely* human or natural processes, thus indicating the mistake of human self-credit for divine *agapē*. God, in short, can "prove" God's reality and worthiness of worship with God's perfect character and will. (The term "prove" is inferior to the term "self-authenticate" here, but at times it may be used, very cautiously, more loosely than is common in mathematics and logic.)

We should expect personal self-authentication from a morally perfect God seeking human redemption. After all, there seems to be nothing else as morally great as God to authenticate divine reality. That is, we have no clear alternative for a source of authentication for this unique God. This consideration fits with the following question of Isaiah 40:25: "To whom then will you compare me, or who is my equal?, says the Holy One." It also fits with the report of Isaiah 44:24–26: "I am the Lord … who confirms the word of his servant, and fulfills the predictions of his messengers." Likewise, it fits with Isaiah 45:22–23: "I am God, and there is no other. By *myself* I have sworn" (italics added). Even if one deploys an abductive argument in support of divine reality, the foundational evidence includes *de re* confrontation with a morally perfect character and will. More accurately, the confrontation is *de te*, owing to its being I–*Thou*, given that God is an intentional agent and not a mere thing.

One can *claim* a fictional object to be self-authenticating, but a mere claim does not evidence make. (We cannot generate evidence or defeaters of evidence quite so easily, and this is a good thing for the pursuit of well-founded true beliefs.) The critical question concerns the evidence for the reality of the corresponding moral character and will. Nothing like the good power of *agapē* has been poured out in receptive human wills by a fictional object, and nothing like divine corrective inquiry or reciprocity is found in the human experience of a fictional object. Arguably, then, the God of *agapē* is unique, and the remaining question is whether we inquirers are sincerely welcoming toward this God, on God's redemptive terms.

We now move, for the better, from anything like traditional natural theology to existential, profoundly volitional epistemology, the epistemology of Gethsemane. We also move beyond any familiar appeal to spectator "miracles" to make a case for God. Let's consider these two traditional alternatives, with attention to their neglecting divine volitional severity in the genuine evidence for God. We shall see that in being self-authenticating God would challenge a person's will and therefore not offer considerations for mere reflection, speculation, observation, or entertainment. That is, God would not use spectator evidence for self-authentication.

Miraculous signs

Luke's Gospel portrays Jesus as offering an austere response to people who seek a particular kind of sign of God, at least in his ministry:

When the crowds were increasing, he [Jesus] began to say, "This generation is an evil generation; it seeks a sign, but no sign shall be given to it except the sign of Jonah. For as Jonah became a sign to the men of Nineveh, so will the Son of man be to this generation … The men of Nineveh will arise at the judgment with this generation and condemn it; for they repented at the preaching of Jonah, and behold, something greater than Jonah is here." (Luke 11:29–32, RSV; cf. Matt. 12:38–40)

Mark's Gospel reports a similar situation where Jesus responds simply that no sign will be given to this generation (Mark 8:11–12).

The "sign" sought by the audience of Jesus was a *miraculous* sign (as indicated in some English translations, such as the NIV translations of Luke 11:29, Matthew 12:38, and Mark 8:12). Accordingly, Jesus suggests that the seeking of miraculous signs, at least with regard to his own status and ministry, is "evil." What does this lesson hold for the relation of miracles to the available evidence for God? In particular, what role, if any, do miracles have in a case for belief in God? Let's proceed with the general notion of a miracle as an *extraordinary* divine intervention, thus allowing for the constancy of divine intervention without our corresponding knowledge of such constancy.

The previous quotation from Luke's Gospel does not refuse miraculous signs altogether. On the contrary, it acknowledges a miraculous "sign" provided *by Jesus himself* in a manner analogous to Jonah's relation to the people of Nineveh. The idea offered is that Jesus is a sign to his generation in a manner analogous to Jonah's being a sign to the people of Nineveh. More specifically, the key point emerges from the claim that the people of Nineveh "repented at the preaching of Jonah, and behold, something greater than Jonah is here" in the person of Jesus. The sign of Jonah, in other words, involves the repentance of Nineveh at his preaching, and this redemptive sign has an analogue in the sign of Jesus to his generation.

The straightforward inference is that just as Jonah was a miraculous sign to Nineveh in virtue of Nineveh's repentance at his preaching, so also Jesus is a miraculous sign from God to his generation. The view that Jesus is such a sign is endorsed in John's Gospel after some people ask him, "What sign do you do, that we may see, and believe you?" (John 6:30, RSV). Of course, many people do not acknowledge Jesus as such a sign, and this leads John's Gospel to offer an explanation: "Everyone who has heard and learned from the Father comes to me [= Jesus]" (John 6:45, RSV). The explanation suggests that being receptive to (learning from) God is central to recognizing Jesus as a miraculous sign from God. Accordingly, John's Gospel states: "If anyone wills to do [God's] will, he will know whether the teaching [of Jesus] is from God" (John 7:17). We should acknowledge the neglected importance of the clause "if anyone wills to do [God's] will." It leads to a sound epistemology of God, a Gethsemane-oriented epistemology.

Two questions emerge. First, what exactly does Jesus's being a miraculous sign from God consist in? Second, exactly how does one's willing to do God's will enable one to discern Jesus's being a sign from God? The latter question involves the issue of what exactly people are to learn from God. Let's briefly consider these important questions.

Kingdom signs

Jonah's being a miraculous sign consists in his central role in the repentance of the people of Nineveh. Specifically, via Jonah's message of judgment on Nineveh, the king of Nineveh brought the following message to his people: "let man and beast be covered with sackcloth, and let them cry mightily to God; yea, let everyone turn from his evil way and from the violence which is in his hands. Who knows, God may yet repent and turn from his fierce anger, so that we perish not?" (Jon. 3:8–9, RSV). Through his message of prospective judgment from God, Jonah became, with the unintended aid of the king, an agent of repentance toward God for the people of Nineveh. When God saw the repentance of the people of Nineveh, he had mercy on them in his "steadfast love" and called off the judgment proclaimed by Jonah (Jon. 3:10, 4:2). Accordingly, Jonah was (if despite his own superficial intentions) a living and breathing sign of God's merciful love that calls for human repentance.

Like Jonah, Jesus was a living, personified sign of divine love that seeks human repentance for the sake of a right relationship with God. Even so, there was a big difference: Jesus *willingly* portrayed the divine message for humans, whereas the message came through Jonah despite his unwilling attitude and behavior. If Jonah is the paradigmatic disobedient prophet used by God, Jesus is the model obedient prophet who carries out God's redemptive mission to humans. Both prophets, however, took their divine message beyond the Jewish people to the Gentile outsiders. Even if Jesus focused his mission on the people of Israel (see Matt. 15:24), he extended his mission to the Gentiles too (see, for instance, Matt. 15:28, Luke 7:1–10). This extended mission became a matter of controversy among some Jews early in the ministry of Jesus (see Luke 4:23–28), and the subsequent controversy over Paul's Gentile mission became a hallmark of his ministry (see, for instance, his letters to the Galatians and the Philippians).

A theme common to all of the New Testament Gospels is that Jesus performed remarkable signs of various sorts. (For classifications of these signs, see Richardson 1941; 1958, pp. 95–102.) According to Matthew's Gospel, some critics of Jesus attributed some of his powerful signs, particularly his exorcisms, to the power of Satan (Matt. 9:34, 12:24–27; cf. Luke 11:15, John 7:20–21, 8:48–54,

11:47–48). As suggested by Luke's and Matthew's Gospels, Jesus offered a contrary source: "if it is by the finger of God that I cast out demons, then the kingdom of God has come upon you" (Luke 11:20; cf. Matt. 12:28). According to all strata of the Gospel traditions, including the so-called "Q" tradition of materials common to Luke and Matthew but not Mark, Jesus performed remarkable signs, and these signs attracted the attention of critics and supporters. We can dispute the source of these signs – God, Satan, or some purely natural source – but the extensive reports of them do call for some explanation.

If Jesus refused a sign to people seeking a sign, as in Luke 11:29–32, why does he reportedly include a wide range of signs in his ministry? Is there an inconsistency here? An important consideration, at least for various New Testament writers, is that Jesus came as the divinely anointed one who was promised in parts of the Hebrew scriptures, including the book of Isaiah (29:18–19, 35:5–6, 61:1–2), as God's redeeming representative. As E. P. Sanders notes, however: "Jesus's actual claim may have been in fact higher [than a claim merely to being God's promised 'Messiah']: not only spokesman for, but viceroy of, God; and not just in a political kingdom but in the kingdom of God" (1993, p. 242; cf. Sanders 1985, pp. 321–322).

Matthew's Gospel portrays Jesus as summing up the pertinent redemptive signs as follows:

Jesus answered them, "Go and tell John [the baptizer] what you hear and see: the blind receive their sight and the lame walk, lepers are cleansed and the deaf hear, and the dead are raised up, and the poor have the good news [prophesied by Isaiah] preached to them. And blessed is he who takes no offense at me." (Matt. 11:4–6, RSV; cf. Luke 4:18–19)

The answer from Jesus suggests that his miracles are signs not only of God's power but also of his own distinctive role in the coming of God's kingship, or reign, on earth. This fits with his controversial preaching that inaugurated his ministry: "The time is fulfilled, and the kingdom of God is at hand; repent, and believe in the gospel" (Mark 1:15, RSV; cf. Matt. 4:17). Accordingly, in these Gospels, Jesus indicates that the kingship of God is drawing near in his own ministry (see Luke 11:20, cited previously).

The signs of Jesus are not impartial, transparent "proofs" of his distinctive status or of God's reality. Instead, they are elusive and subtle indicators of the power of God in his life and mission. This raises the question of what God aims to accomplish with such elusive signs. Particularly, what does God want us to learn from Jesus and perhaps from Jonah too, if Jesus and Jonah are themselves elusive signs from God? Let's approach this issue indirectly, by considering the human failure to perceive God's signs.

Willing and discerning

Many people deny that Jesus Christ is a sign from God, and they demand a sign of some distinctive sort to buttress any claim that Jesus is a genuine sign from God. In doing so, they suggest that Jesus himself was and is an inadequate sign from God, if he was such a sign at all. By way of response, Alan Richardson comments:

It is possible for us to fail to see Christ as the manifestation of the power and the purpose of God; then we shall be content with an explanation of the miracle-stories in terms of modern psychology or folk-mythology. The miracle-stories, as an essential part of the preaching of apostolic Christianity, confront us with the question whether the power of God was or was not revealed in the person and work of Jesus Christ. They compel us to say Yes or No. (1941, p. 126)

Of course, a person can plead ignorance, but the question remains of whether Jesus himself is a sign of the power and the purpose of God. Some people answer negatively, but this is premature in advance of clarification of the talk of "the power and the purpose of God." It is akin to denying God's existence without a clear understanding of what the exalted title "God" actually involves, and this is an occupational hazard among philosophers and other theorists.

According to Richardson, "to understand the meaning of the miracle-stories of the Gospel tradition it is first necessary to have penetrated the incognito of Jesus, and to have seen behind the Jesus of Galilee the Christ of New Testament faith" (1941, p. 137). This may be so, but we still need clarification of the relevant talk of the power, purpose, and meaning of God in the signs under consideration. We also need clarification of what is involved in "the Christ of New Testament faith."

Richardson explains:

[Jesus] was not concerned to impress his contemporaries with his marvelous power; but rather ... he asked them by the same token to believe that he had authority upon earth to forgive sins. He not merely opened the eyes of blind men, but claimed by that sign the power to make men see the truth of God ... And, finally, he not merely raised a child or a man from the dead, but claimed in doing so to be the resurrection and the life ... In the last resort it was the sign of the resurrection which authenticated all Jesus's other signs and the claims which they involved. (1941, pp. 131–132; cf. John 2:18–22)

Richardson points us in the direction suggested by Jesus himself (see Mark 2:9–11; cf. Luke 5:22–24). Note, however, the initial oddness of invoking the resurrection of Jesus as what "authenticated" the signs and claims of Jesus. The problem is that his resurrection is not shared evidence, let alone a transparent "proof," for all parties to the dispute. Indeed, one's invoking the resurrection of Jesus will seem question-begging at best to most critics.

Evidence regarding the resurrection of Jesus seems sensitive to an inquirer's will (relative to God's will) in a manner that challenges its being used as a transparent authentication for all concerned. Jesus himself apparently acknowledged as much, in ascribing the following remark to Abraham in a parabolic story: "If they do not listen to Moses and the prophets, neither will they be convinced even if someone rises from the dead" (Luke 16:31). This remark is arguably an important indicator of the epistemology of Jesus himself, and it speaks against any kind of simple historical empiricism as a means for adjudicating the resurrection of Jesus or related divine signs. One's listening to Moses and the prophets somehow figures in one's being suitably convinced of the resurrection. The clarification of "somehow" is, of course, important now.

We can take some steps by attending to the idea of "listening to Moses and the prophets." The natural question is: listening to *what* in Moses and the prophets? Jesus does not have in mind *all* of the details of the Mosaic law and the prophets' teachings. In fact, he corrects some of the teachings of the Hebrew scriptures, including those about God as hating his enemies. For instance, Psalm 11:5 reports: "The Lord tests the righteous and the wicked, and his soul hates him that loves violence" (RSV; cf. Ps. 5:5). In sharp contrast with such teaching of the Hebrew Bible, Jesus taught that God loves evil people, including God's enemies, and that the children of God should follow suit.

Jesus taught as follows in the Sermon on the Mount: "You have heard that it was said, 'You shall love your neighbor and hate your enemy.' But I say to you, Love your enemies and pray for those who persecute you, so that you may be sons of your Father who is in heaven ... You must be perfect, as your heavenly Father is perfect" (Matt. 5:43–45, 48, RSV; cf. Luke 6:27–36, Rom. 12:20–21). Clearly, then, Jesus did not share the hateful attitude of the psalmist or assign that attitude to God. Instead, he attributed enemy-love to God and expected the same love from his followers. (For relevant discussion, see Klassen 1984, chap. 4.)

Jesus thinks of the primary lesson of the Hebrew Bible (including "Moses and the prophets") as pointing to God's redemptive *agapē*, and – here's the rub – he suggested, if elusively, that this *agapē* is humanly personified in himself. This righteous, severe love, according to Jesus, includes definite divine commandments that are to be obeyed wholeheartedly by humans. According to Matthew's Gospel, he portrays "the [Mosaic] law and the prophets" as depending on two commandments: first, the commandment to love the Lord your God with all your heart, soul, and mind; and, second, the commandment to love your neighbor as yourself (22:37–40; cf. Mark 12:29–31). Mark's Gospel portrays Jesus as adding that there is no commandment greater than these two (12:31), and Luke's Gospel represents Jesus as offering these two commandments in response to the question of what one can do to inherit eternal life with God (10:25–28).

Jesus acknowledges that humans do not fully obey the divine love-commandments at the heart of his teaching and therefore need forgiveness and repentance before God. He says of humans: "If you, who are evil, know how to give good gifts to your children, how much more will your Father who is in heaven give good gifts to those who ask him?" (Matt. 7:11). In addition, he remarks, in connection with a question about inheriting eternal life, that "no one is good but God alone" (Mark 10:18, Luke 18:19; cf. Matt. 19:17, John 2:24). As a result, Jesus claims that it is impossible for humans to save themselves, but that human salvation is nonetheless possible for God (see Mark 10:26–27, Luke 18:26–27, Matt. 19:25–26).

Anchoring Paul's message on divine grace, Jesus offers the parable of the laborers in the vineyard to teach that God's kingdom operates by God's gracious generosity rather than by human scales of merit or earning (see Matt. 20:1–16). Moreover, he offers the parable of the Pharisee and the tax collector to illustrate that human justification before God stems from God's mercy rather than human self-righteousness (see Luke 18:9–14). The latter parable nicely grounds Paul's famous message of human redemption by "the free gift of righteousness" from God (see Rom. 5:17; cf. Rom. 3:21–26).

We now may acknowledge that divine love, in the teaching of Jesus, involves a life-giving merciful gift (of right relationship with God) as well as a command (to love God and others). A salient later summary of this position arises in John 3:16: "For God so loved the world that he gave his only Son, [in order] that whoever believes in him should not perish but have eternal life" (RSV). Even if this famous proclamation did not come directly from Jesus himself, it captures the central message of Jesus, and it relates divine love to human faith (to which the next section returns).

The Gospel of John has a special interest in human perceiving and failing to perceive Jesus as the culminating sign of God for human redemption. In John 7:4, the brothers of Jesus say to him: "if you do these things [that is, these signs], show yourself to the world" (RSV). John interjects an editorial remark: "For even his brothers did not believe in him" (John 7:5). He thus suggests that Jesus's brothers were not in a position to understand the nature of his signs, particularly their pointing to a distinctive kind of divine redemptive love. Their charge to "show yourself to the world" manifests a serious misunderstanding of God and Jesus on their part, particularly the redemptive mission of God and Jesus.

Jesus draws a sharp contrast between his brothers and himself, as follows: "The world cannot hate you, but it hates me because I testify of it that its works are evil" (John 7:7). Following this indication of needed repentance before God (with echoes of Jonah), Jesus issues his key cognitive principle: "If anyone wills to do [God's] will, he will know whether the teaching [of mine] is from God or whether I am speaking on my own authority" (John 7:17). One's "willing to do God's will" emerges, then, as significant in discerning whether Jesus is genuinely a sign from God. Being a proposed sign from God in the tradition of Jonah, Jesus seeks a response of human repentance and trust in the light of God's merciful and demanding love. Let's consider the cognitive basis for such a challenging and life-defining response that echoes the crisis of Gethsemane.

FROM *AGAPĒ* TO FAITH

A decisive matter concerns what exactly God wants out of divine signs, including the humanly personified signs of Jonah and Jesus. The case of Jonah illustrates that at a minimum God aims to reveal that God is "gracious … and merciful, slow to anger, and abounding in steadfast love" (Jon. 4:2). In accordance with this aim, God employs Jonah to call the people of Nineveh to repentance and trust toward God, and when they repent, God promptly calls off the judgment threatened by Jonah (3:4–5; 4:2, 11). The sign of Jonah, then, manifests God's "merciful, steadfast love" for the sake of calling wayward people into reconciliation with God. This is the culminating lesson of the book of Jonah (4:11), and Jesus found it to anticipate his own ministry on behalf of God toward wayward humans.

Like Jonah, Jesus regarded himself as one sent by God to manifest, in his life and his death, God's merciful, steadfast love toward wayward people. Accordingly, Luke portrays Jesus as proclaiming, "Fear not, little flock, for it is your Father's good pleasure to give you the [divine] kingdom" (Luke 12:32). God's merciful, unearned giving of his kingdom, through Jesus, to wayward people is his "grace," in Paul's influential language (see Rom. 3:21–26). This language of "grace" (*charis*) is a simple variation on the language of divine *agapē*, or self-giving, merciful righteous *love* even toward God's enemies (see Robinson 1904, pp. 224–226). The heart of the matter, according to various New Testament writers, is that God "first loved us," apart from what we merit (see 1 John 4:19; cf. 1 John 4:10, Rom. 5:8, 10).

The redemptive love manifested by God in the living signs of Jonah and Jesus is not only offered to humans by God but also, as suggested, commanded by God of potential recipients of divine love. Even so, we should not think of the divine love-commands as requiring that humans produce unselfish love on their own. Leon Morris correctly notes: "The love that is commanded [by God] is not a love that believers generate themselves; it is a love that proceeds from divine love. Confronted with God's love, we may respond by accepting it or rejecting it" (1981, p. 189; cf. Nygren 1953, pp. 125–126). Accordingly, we must face the question of how humans are to appropriate the divine love on offer. If such love is integral to the signs offered in Jonah and Jesus, we should also ask, in the same vein, how humans are to appropriate the divine signs on offer. The fact that this love is an unmerited gift to humans is perfectly compatible with its being appropriated in struggle and severity.

A familiar story is that the things of God, including divine signs, are to be received *by faith*, or by *people of faith*. This story may be defensible ultimately, but it demands clarification of its slippery talk of *faith*. The idea and the phenomenon of faith certainly loom large in the ministry of Jesus and, subsequently, in the mission of Paul to the Gentiles. In modern times, however, the idea of faith has become polluted by fideism, the troubled view that religious belief is exempt from the demands of evidence or cognitive support of any kind. A misreading of Kierkegaard (under his pseudonyms) has contributed to such distortion among contemporary philosophers and theologians (on which see Moser and McCreary 2010; cf. Moser 2010a, chap. 2), but an antidote is available in some of the New Testament writings. The needed antidote, however, is one of the best-kept secrets in philosophical theology and in New Testament studies.

Paul comments as follows on the relation between faith and love: "In Christ Jesus neither circumcision nor uncircumcision is of any avail, but faith working through love" (Gal. 5:6, RSV). The RSV margin of this translation fittingly notes that the alternative translation of the relevant participle *energoumené* in the passive instead of middle voice leaves us with "faith *made effective* through love." (In favor of the passive rendering, particularly "*made operative* through love," see Robinson 1904, pp. 241–247; Duncan 1934, pp. 157–158; and Clark 1935.) Duncan recommends that we should read Galatians 5:6 "in the clear light of Galatians 2:20, where … Paul declares that what brought him to rest exclusively on *faith* was the revelation of a Saviour who *loved* him" (1934, p. 157). In Paul's Good News proclamation: "I have been crucified with Christ; it is no longer I who live, but Christ who lives in me; and the life I now live in the flesh I live by faith in the Son of God, who loved me and gave himself for me" (Gal. 2:20, RSV). Evidently, Paul thought of his faith as based in divine self-giving love manifested in God's Son, Jesus Christ.

We need not digress to a debate about the middle or passive voice of the participle *energoumené* in Galatians 5:6. Even if one favors the middle voice and opts for "faith expressing itself through love" (as many contemporary translators and commentators do), one still needs to identify the ultimate source of the love in question. Paul is altogether clear on this source (cf. Spicq 1965, p. 222), as we have noted on the basis of Romans 5:1, 3–5:

Since we are justified by faith, we have peace with God through our Lord Jesus Christ … And not only that, but we also boast in our sufferings, knowing that suffering produces endurance, and endurance produces character, and character produces hope, and hope does not disappoint us, because God's love (*agapē*) has been poured into our hearts through the Holy Spirit that has been given to us. (cf. 2 Cor. 5:5, 14).

The key phrase is "God's love has been poured into our hearts."

Paul understands hope in God as including faith in God directed toward the future when God will fulfill a divine promise, and he therefore uses "faith" and "hope" interchangeably at times (on which see Brunner 1962, pp. 339–346; Ridderbos 1975, pp. 248–252). As suggested, then, Paul also would say that faith in God "does not disappoint us, because God's love has been poured into our hearts." This consideration fits well with Paul's mention of "faith" (in God) at the opening of the previous quotation, in Romans 5:1.

We now may endorse Emil Brunner's perceptive observation that "faith [in God] is nothing other than the vessel into which God pours his love ... Faith is ... the openness of our heart for God's love" (1957, p. 75; cf. p. 33). Brunner speaks fittingly of "the faith [in God] which consists in the reception of the divine love" (1962, p. 236; cf. p. 316). This divinely intended connection between divine love and human faith in God bears directly on the purpose and the cognitive status of divine signs, including those found elusively in Jonah and Jesus.

The redemptive God worthy of worship does not seek human faith, belief, or knowledge regarding God apart from (divinely intended) transformative human reception of divine love. In other words, God does not offer signs to prompt human faith based *just* on intellectual reflections or any other factors apart from the transformative human reception of divine love. Human faith in God, we might say, is not faith merely in God's existence; it is faith in *God*, including God's perfect moral character and will. Accordingly, contrary to the attitudes of many philosophers, divine signs are not offered as the stuff of a spectator sport or an intellectual quiz.

Genuine divine signs come with the divine aim to redirect human wills away from the futility of selfishness, pride, and despair and toward life in full, reverent cooperation and companionship with

God. Such signs, then, will not serve their divine purpose of the volitional transformation of humans, or even be perceived by humans for what they truly are, if they are not willingly received, in repentance and trust toward God, as a source of divine transformative love. That is, they are divinely intended as a means of new, cooperative life with God, in keeping with God's perfect character and will. We might say, then, that they come with a life-or-death challenge to humans – hardly the stuff of casual intellectual entertainment.

N. R. Hanson comments: "There is no single natural happening, nor any constellation of such happenings, which establishes God's existence … If the heavens cracked open and [a] Zeus-like figure … made his presence and nature known to the world, *that* would establish such a happening" (1971, p. 322). This reveals a serious misunderstanding of divine signs, and the misunderstanding is widely shared among philosophers and others. It is not clear what Hanson means by "natural happening," and it is doubtful that we should expect God to be available in purely "natural" happenings. In any case, it is unclear that Hanson's imagined Zeus intervention would have anything to do with *God's* robust existence and character. As suggested in Chapter 1, the term "God" is a maximally exalted title requiring worthiness of worship, but Hanson's Zeus appears to be nothing more than an object of entertainment for casual spectators. In particular, there is nothing redemptive about this Zeus-like figure in the face of human selfishness, pride, hate, despair, superficiality, and self-destruction. Hanson's imagined case therefore does not bring us anywhere near *God* as worthy of worship, even if suggests an amusing false god.

We now can break with any kind of fideism regarding the divine signs of Jonah and Jesus as well as human faith in God. God's love being poured into our hearts is no mere belief; it is a salient *experience* that serves as the cognitive, evidential foundation of well-founded belief in God (on which see Moser 2008, 2010a, 2010b). As Brunner notes, "[Divine] love is the criterion by which we recognize whether our faith is genuine faith … (Gal. 5:6). For faith [in God] is not mere knowledge; it is [the human reception of] the self-communication of the divine life, the love which manifests itself as the principle of the new life" (1962, p. 339). The human reception of such divine love is a rigorous struggle to receive (as an unmerited gift) God's perfect character of love and thereby to trust God. This is very different from any spectator experience of a Zeus-like figure who cracks open the heavens and leaves us morally unchallenged and unchanged. We have here a salient difference between God as worthy of worship and a false god.

WITHOUT NATURAL THEOLOGY

Our lesson regarding miracles and *agapē* extends to the traditional arguments of natural theology. John's Gospel portrays Jesus as offering the following critical remark:

> Truly, truly, you seek me, not because you saw [kingdom] signs, but because you ate your fill of the loaves. Do not labor for the food which perishes, but for the food which endures to eternal life, which the Son of man will give to you; for on him has God the Father set his seal. (John 6:26–27, RSV)

According to John's Gospel, God cares about human motives in seeking and believing regarding God.

John's Gospel suggests that God cares about how a person fills in the following blank: "I inquire or believe regarding God's existence because I want —." As a result, we should begin by asking what human motive(s) God would want to underlie human inquiry and belief regarding God. This strategic lesson is widely neglected among philosophers, theologians, and others, but it can illumin-ate a religious epistemology suited to a God worthy of worship. In particular, as we shall see, this lesson can highlight the shortcomings of the arguments of traditional natural theology.

What has traditional natural theology to do with faith in the God who merits worship? Such natural theology offers arguments, in *a priori* and *a posteriori* forms, for the conclusion that God exists, and some of these arguments have been highly influential in many movements and eras. They include various ontological, contingency, cosmological, teleological, moral, and psychological arguments, among others, and the pertinent details can be remarkably elaborate. (For specific shortcomings of these arguments, see Moser 2010a, chap. 3.) We shall see that such arguments fail to accommodate the motive(s) that God, as worthy of worship, would want in human inquiry and belief regarding God. This God, according to this section, does not need the arguments of natural theology and is not the god represented by such arguments. The God worthy of worship, in other words, is not the god of the philosophers' arguments of traditional natural theology.

Philosophers and theologians do not all mean the same thing by "natural theology." Some have in mind any theological information or beliefs independent of scripture (or "special revelation"), whereas some others have in mind theological arguments of a certain sort that are independent of scripture (or "special revelation"). James Barr offers the following characterization:

Traditionally "natural theology" has commonly meant something like this: that "by nature," that is, just by being human beings, men and women have a certain degree of knowledge of God and awareness of him, or at least a capacity for such an awareness; and this knowledge exists anterior to the special revelation of God made through Jesus Christ, through the Church, through the Bible. (1993, p. 1)

This characterization is very broad in that it does not require of natural theology any arguments for God's existence, certainly not the traditional arguments for God's existence. This section works with a narrower conception of natural theology because it understands "natural theology" to rely on (a variation of) at least one of the aforementioned traditional arguments for God's existence.

Barr's characterization mentions "a certain degree of knowledge of God and awareness of him, or at least a capacity for such an awareness" independent of "special revelation" from God through Jesus, the Christian church, and the Bible. This is vague talk because it does not indicate whether the relevant knowledge of God has certain propositional content, such as the content that God exists. Initially, one might think that the relevant knowledge requires a direct awareness of God, regardless of the propositional content one accepts. This would be mistaken, however, because the characterization allows for just "a capacity" for awareness of God, and such a capacity does not require actual awareness of God. Accordingly, Barr's characterization is unacceptably vague. We can remove the vagueness by requiring of natural theology reliance on (a variation of) at least one of the aforementioned traditional arguments for God's existence.

The arguments of natural theology seek to establish, or at least to confirm, God's existence on the basis of *natural* sources of human evidence and knowledge, without an appeal to a special revelation from God. If an argument appeals to a special revelation from God, it arguably qualifies as an argument of *supernatural* theology rather than of natural theology. The distinction between what is natural and what is supernatural may not be altogether clear, but we can exclude from what is natural at least a direct word from God or a word from God through God's prophets. Traditional natural theology proceeds with this exclusion, and we may follow suit.

Proponents of natural theology should note that we have no distinctively *Jewish–Christian* natural theology that concludes with the claim that the Jewish–Christian God exists. The lack of a distinctively Jewish–Christian natural theology suggests, or arguably should suggest, that the distinctive features of the Jewish–Christian God demand more than what we humans can confirm by our natural sources of information. I take this suggestion seriously and will contend that traditional natural theology is inadequate and dispensable relative to the evidential standard and resources for the God worthy of worship.

If an argument is to establish the existence of the Jewish–Christian God, it must establish the existence of a *personal, intentional agent worthy of worship*. Worthiness of worship is, of course, no small matter, even if it is hard to find in human experience. It requires worthiness of full, unqualified commitment, because worship requires full, unqualified commitment. In addition, one will be worthy of full, unqualified commitment only if one is self-sufficiently morally perfect, without any defect. Moral defectiveness, such as selfishness or pride, undermines worthiness of full commitment and therefore precludes worthiness of worship. As a result, given the title "God" as used in central parts of Jewish–Christian monotheism, God's character must be free of selfishness and characterized by unselfish righteous love, or *agapē*, toward all persons, even toward enemies of God. The title "God" is, as Chapter 1 suggested, a maximally exalted title regarding a perfect moral character that is self-sufficient.

Advocates of natural theology have the massive burden of establishing via an argument limited to natural sources of evidence that a personal agent worthy of worship exists. None of the arguments of natural theology, however, enjoys widespread support as having actually discharged this burden. We can characterize the history of natural theology as the history of attempting to secure knowledge of God's reality solely via natural sources of evidence, without acknowledging direct evidence of God's authoritative call to humans. Let's consider some broad but conclusive reasons why this widely influential attempt fails and will continue to fail.

Suppose that the evidence offered by traditional natural theology is *spectator* evidence because it makes no demand on the human will to cooperate with God's will and involves only *de dicto*, and not *de re*, content regarding God. (This captures the core of spectator evidence as I understand it.) If one proceeds with just such evidence, one will fall short of evidence for a God worthy of worship. In that case, one will lack evidence for a *de re* personal intervention by God and for a corresponding command from God. We should expect, however, a truly redemptive God to intervene *de re* in human lives, for the sake of challenging and inviting humans to a new life in cooperation with God.

Given only *de dicto* evidence, one will lack evidence for the God worthy of worship, even if one has evidence for the god of deism or the god of the philosophers. It is no surprise, then, that contemporary debates over the arguments of natural theology rarely, if ever, get around to the crucial redemptive features to be expected of a God worthy of worship. Here is the real danger of natural theology: it leaves us, from the standpoint of redemption, in an optional intellectual sideshow, without pointing us to (the salient evidence for) the redemptive moral character of the God worthy of worship.

Many philosophers of religion worry that some kind of natural theological argument is needed *prior* to a person's willingness to consider receiving a direct volitional challenge from God. In this perspective, God would have to rely on some kind of natural theological argument to challenge beliefs unfriendly to endorsing and cooperating with God's existence. This view is mistaken. Humanly available *de re* experience and evidence of God can undermine the relevant unfriendly beliefs by supplying defeaters, particularly undefeated defeaters. An experience of divine corrective inquiry in conscience, for instance, could supply a relevant defeater. God, then, would not have to wait for one to deliberate on and change one's anti-God beliefs by *independent*, natural theological arguments. In addition, God could present both *de re* evidence of God's moral character and personal assurance of God's moral perfection via divine corrective inquiry and reciprocity, without the arguments of natural theology. We have no good reason to suppose otherwise.

Consider Abraham, Isaac, and Jacob in relation to the intervening God, Yahweh. They did not have to wait for Plato, Aristotle, or Anselm to develop natural theology as a means to their knowledge of God. In addition, their knowledge of God was existentially and redemptively significant, owing to divine corrective reciprocity, rather than to abstract philosophical considerations. God provided the needed evidence directly, or so one could argue abductively, given my account. Accordingly, merely *de dicto* natural theological arguments are dispensable for knowledge of God, even if they happen to have some psychological value for some people in some situations. It is doubtful, then, that the spectator evidence offered by the arguments of traditional natural theology is cognitively needed as a preliminary or an accompaniment to human knowledge of God.

A case for natural theology sometimes rests on a demand for a certain kind of evidence of God that seems to be unavailable to humans. One variation on this demand requires that any awareness of God's character that qualifies as evidence of God must yield one's having defensible answers to skeptical questions about God's existence. The latter requirement, however, is too demanding. One's *having* conclusive evidence of God does not entail one's having a propositional answer to a question about God or any alternative to God. It would be a dubious kind of level-confusion to suggest otherwise: a confusion of the conditions for one's *having* evidence and the conditions for one's *showing*, *giving*, or *presenting* evidence in answer to a question or challenge. That confusion makes one's having evidence overly intellectual, and invites a kind of regress problem. A theory falls prey to that defect whenever the conditions for answering questions become necessary conditions for one's simply having evidence.

Answers to questions are propositional; evidence need not be, and foundational evidence is not. Questions about our "answering questions" typically concern our *showing*, *giving*, or *presenting* evidence, in addition to our offering true answers. The latter concern is more intellectual and reflective than the more basic conditions for one's having evidence (for elaboration, see Moser 1989, 2008). In this connection, it is a serious mistake to assume that mere doxastic diversity or disagreement, even among one's peers, yields a defeater for the relevant belief in God. Mere disagreement is akin to mere belief in lacking the evidential status to generate an epistemic defeater. Otherwise, we could produce defeaters at will, but that would rob evidence of its distinctive status. Many philosophers neglect this basic point about defeaters.

Some inquirers might have misgivings about the proposed *de re* salient evidence in human experience of divine *agapē*, on the ground that we humans are laden with selfishness and pride. I have no brief against the reality of our moral defectiveness in this regard, but this defectiveness can be a distorting human overlay on God's gift of *agapē*, freely added by imperfect humans. Life with God, therefore, could include a human struggle to remove this defective overlay for the sake of revealing the underlying gift received. In addition, God could allow for human freedom not only to receive this gift, but also to reject it, even after receiving it initially.

A truly redemptive God would seek to hold together, in actual human lives, *de re* and *de dicto* evidence of God, for the sake of the moral transformation of humans toward divine *agapē* and forgiveness, even for one's enemies. That is, God would aim to combine humans' *knowing God* with humans' knowing that God exists. As a result, reflection on God would be offered not as a spectator sport but instead as a life-forming challenge from the morally authoritative presence of God. This would result from the reality of divine corrective inquiry and reciprocity. God's self-authenticating evidence would aim to yield new, God-directed life in humans.

God does not have to postpone a Gethsemane context and its needed redemptive benefits for humans until the philosophical theologians weigh in with their arguments. This is an important cognitive and redemptive fact, given the esoteric and indecisive nature of the typical arguments of natural theology. A redemptive God would offer a new, humanly experienced dimension of volitional cooperation and companionship with God that overcomes the endless doubts prompted by much philosophy of religion. This would involve divine corrective inquiry and reciprocity, and it is part of what Paul calls God's "new creation" and contrasts with "knowing according to flesh" (see 2 Cor. 5:16–17). Evidently, some humans prefer endless philosophical debate as an alternative to God's new creation in divine corrective reciprocity, but this is a serious mistake in priorities. (On the important idea of new creation in Paul, see Hubbard 2002.)

Jesus and Paul could have used arguments from natural theology to make their case on behalf of the Jewish–Christian God, but they did not take that option. Paul, in particular, presented his case for the Jewish–Christian God before Epicurean and Stoic philosophers in Athens, but he did not resort to any argument of natural theology (see Acts 17:18–34). If the arguments of natural theology were important to the case for the Jewish–Christian God, they would likely emerge at least in outline somewhere in the Jewish–Christian scriptures, but they do not. This is telling indeed, and often neglected by proponents of the arguments of natural theology.

According to the message of various New Testament writers, God's distinctive moral character is imaged perfectly in the evidence representing who Jesus Christ is as an intentional agent with definite gifts, demands, and goals from God himself. (Chapter 5 returns to this theme.) As this message shows, God did not send humans just additional information or more laws or arguments. Instead, God sent revelatory personifying evidence in Jesus Christ and thereby in the followers of Jesus who are being conformed to his *agapē*-oriented moral image that reflects God. We can find analogues of this lesson in the earlier Jewish history and elsewhere.

John's Gospel portrays Jesus as saying that people will know his disciples by the intentional *agapē* they manifest in themselves for one another, after the pattern of Jesus's *agapē* (see John 13:35). A cognitive role for *agapē* also emerges in the following striking remark in 1 John 4:7–16: "let us love one another; for love (*agapē*) is of God, and he who loves is born of God and knows God. He who does not love does not know God; for God is love" (RSV). Similarly, we have noted well a cognitive role for *agapē* in the following remark by Paul: "hope [in God] does not disappoint us, because God's love (*agapē*) has been poured into our hearts through the Holy Spirit ... given to us" (Rom. 5:5). (For relevant discussion, see Gorman 2001, chap. 8; 2009, chap. 2; Moser 2008, chap. 2; 2010a, chap. 4.)

Some philosophers and theologians portray the apostle Paul as an advocate of an argument of natural theology, given his remarks in Romans 1:19–20. This is a serious mistake. Paul does not claim that nature *alone* reveals, establishes, or otherwise confirms divine reality; nor does he argue for God's existence on the basis of certain features of nature. In particular, he does not offer a cosmological or a teleological argument for God's existence. Instead, Paul explicitly claims that "*God* has shown" divine reality to people (Rom. 1:19), even if through nature. This, of course, is not equivalent to a claim about divine revelation "through nature *alone*." If he were inclined to present an argument of natural theology, Paul easily could have claimed that nature *by itself* manifests God's reality, but he definitely does not suggest this in any way.

We should observe a simple distinction between God's being revealed "through nature" and God's being revealed "in nature by itself." As Hendrikus Berkhof remarks, "Nature in itself does not reveal God. [God] reveals Himself in history through his words and deeds" (1968, p. 52). This is an important correction for much of traditional natural theology. An analogy can help. When I call my friend on the phone, the phone itself is not evidence of my existence for my friend. My voice, however, could supply such evidence for my friend. In other words, my existence is not revealed in the phone by itself but it can be revealed *through* the phone (as a medium) as I speak to my friend, say, as I call out my friend's name.

In Romans 1, Paul assumes that *God's showing* what can be known of God to humans includes God's showing his being worthy of honor, thanksgiving, and even worship (see Rom. 1:21, 25). On this ground, rather than on the basis of an argument of natural theology, Paul infers that people who resist worship of God are "without excuse" (Rom. 1:20). *God* still must show people God and call people to God via self-manifestation, because nature does not do this by itself, even if God sometimes uses it as a medium. In that case, natural theological arguments from nature alone will not deliver a personal God worthy of worship.

Clearly, the First Cause/Designer of traditional natural theology could be morally evil, but God, by normative title, could not be. So, we should avoid any familiar inference from the former to the latter. In fact, I have suggested that one cannot get there (to a God worthy of worship) from here (the merely natural premises of the traditional empirical arguments). The heart of the problem is that one cannot get from here to God's personal, intentional moral character of perfection and hence cannot get to a God worthy of worship. Arguably, we have to learn that God is the Creator by God's *de re* testimony, after we learn of God's moral character in a Gethsemane context. Analogously, ancient Hebraic knowledge of God as the Creator arguably arose after knowledge of God as the Exodus rescuer. I see no way to argue otherwise without inviting big problems of the kind facing the arguments of traditional natural theology (see further Moser 2010a, chap. 3).

Seeking to redeem humans, the God worthy of worship would have a specific purpose different from our casually knowing that God exists, via volitionally unchallenging spectator evidence. (As noted, spectator evidence, unlike divine authoritative evidence, does not challenge one to conform to God's morally perfect will.) The redemptive purpose of the God worthy of worship would be to bring humans into lasting reconciliation with God, in loving and obedient companionship with God. Accordingly, we should expect God to offer purposively available evidence of God's reality that promotes this redemptive purpose. It is doubtful that the alleged spectator evidence of traditional natural theology serves such a purpose, because such evidence does not engage us with a challenge to our tendencies that need redemption by God's power. In particular, such alleged evidence does not challenge us to undergo transformation toward God's loving character and away from our selfishness. In other words, it does not encourage us, ourselves, to become personifying evidence of God by reflecting God's moral character, inwardly and outwardly.

The role of God's concern about human motives in inquiry and belief regarding God admits of straightforward elaboration by way of contrast with natural theology. The transformative motives sought by God in human inquiry and belief regarding God include primarily human love for God and human trust, or faith, in God, for the sake of lasting companionship with God and all receptive humans. As a result, God's aim would be to exclude such motives as human selfish fear, self-righteous pride, and *purely* alethic or cognitive interest in human inquiry and belief regarding God. The arguments of traditional natural theology are no help here, and are often counterproductive relative to this redemptive aim.

In the best interest of humans, God would seek a morally profound motive for humans and therefore would not settle for pure, morally indifferent truth-seeking or knowledge-seeking. Truth-seeking and knowledge-seeking have an important role in God's redemptive plan, but they do not capture by themselves the kind of redemptive transformation of humans sought by the God worthy of worship. Such transformation includes humans, themselves, becoming personifying evidence of God's moral character and reality, for the sake of realizing in actual human lives God's noncoercive kingdom of *agapē* toward all agents. God's intended redemption is fully person-involving in this manner. In other words, it is fully participatory and incarnational.

My case against traditional natural theology relies on an understanding of the title "God" in terms of a personal agent worthy of worship, in accordance with Chapter 1 (and in accordance with a central strand of Jewish–Christian monotheism). Someone might wonder whether this case itself is a variation on traditional natural theology. It is not, however, because it does not offer, just on the basis of natural sources of knowledge, an inference to the existence of a supernatural being. My case relies on a notion of God, as a personal agent worthy of worship, but this notion does not figure in an argument for God's existence from purely natural sources of information. As a result, we do not need to rely on an argument of natural theology to challenge natural theology.

Regarding the source of the relevant *notion* of God, this book contends that it emerges for humans in human struggle with the title-holder of "God," that is, the God worthy of worship. This lesson is not an antecedent assumption that threatens to make the present case circular; instead, it arises from the case under development here. We should not confuse, however, the conditions for the *origin* of a concept for humans and the conditions for reasonable belief that the concept stands for an actual entity.

My objection to traditional natural theology does not extend to all cases for God from religious experience. In fact, this book offers one such case, if a neglected case from interventions of *agapē* via corrective inquiry and reciprocity in human experience. As suggested, Romans 5:5 summarizes this book's account, because it offers the humanly experienced flood of divine *agapē* in receptive human persons as the cognitive foundation for hope and faith in God. Arguably, then, Paul was an experiential foundationalist about firsthand evidence and knowledge of God, although most commentators and philosophers fail to understand his distinctive *agapē*-oriented epistemology (see Moser 2010a, chap. 4, for some details).

The details of a robust epistemological alternative to traditional natural theology are available elsewhere (see Moser 2008, 2010a, 2010b), but we should acknowledge that without divine self-revelation the God worthy of worship will not be an object of knowledge for humans. We have no reason to suppose that by means of their own natural sources of evidence humans can acquire knowledge of this God. The more plausible view is that through self-revelation this God must supply for humans the needed evidence of divine reality. This view of divine self-authentication best explains the absence of the arguments of natural theology in the Jewish–Christian scriptures.

We are not left now with fideism, the troubled view that belief in the Jewish–Christian God needs or has no supporting evidence (on which see Moser 2010a, chap. 2, and Moser and McCreary 2010). In providing self-revelation to humans at the opportune times, which are not always times preferred by humans, God shows Godself to be living and faithful, on God's morally profound and challenging terms. Such a self-revelation can yield divine corrective inquiry of humans and thus salient evidence of God for humans.

Alan Richardson explains:

The answer ... to the question why God does not offer proofs of his existence as the sovereign Lord of all things is that he has in fact done so, but only to those who have understood the true nature of kingship. Divine kingship consists not in coercive power but in patient love. God, because he is God, chooses to win man's love where he could have coerced his assent ... God does not want us to believe in him because we have been overawed by his power or impressed by his wonder; he does not want us to give him our allegiance as a result of our misunderstanding of his true nature, so that we should seek him because we desire the material prosperity that might be assured to us by being on the winning side (cf. John 6:26). He wants us to respond to what he is, not to what he is not, and he is the one who loves without asking for reward and who expects us to serve him by loving other people in the same way ... [N]o cosmic demonstration, no metaphysical proof, could elicit the kind of faith which God desires ... To seek any other sign [than divine *agapē*] ... is a seeking after a false image of God, which is idolatry (cf. Matt. 16:4). (1966, pp. 107–108)

Accordingly, the Jewish–Christian God self-manifests, and thereby self-authenticates, with the rare but sacred evidence of self-giving *agapē*, as seen paradigmatically (but not exclusively) in the self-giving life and death of Jesus Christ as God's unique emissary and beloved son. In addition, this God calls humans to become personifying evidence of this God as they learn to (struggle to) receive and reflect God's distinctive moral character.

We can give salient evidence and even sound arguments for God's reality, but they cannot be reduced to any natural theology limited to natural sources of evidence. They need to allow for *supernatural* evidence that comes from the power of a God of self-giving love, and they can recruit abductive, explanatory inference to avoid pointless question begging (see, for example, Moser 2008, chap. 2; 2010a, chap. 4). Even so, any arguments offered will not be themselves the ultimate source of the evidence for God. God's self-revelation will be the needed ultimate source, and given that God is worthy of worship, God's self-revelation will manifest God's character of self-giving love, in keeping with the profound insight that "God is love" (1 John 4:8). In short, God authenticates Godself, with self-manifestation to humans.

Humans can ignore or reject God's self-revelation, but a receptive human motive in inquiry about God will open a door to evidence beyond ordinary imagination and belief and lead beyond divine corrective inquiry to divine corrective reciprocity. The outstanding question is whether humans are willing to open the volitional door to a God of self-giving *agapē*. Much is at risk for familiar human ways. This God, unlike the god of the philosophers, promises to renew everything, including cooperative humans, under the power of *agapē*, and such renewal is rigorous, given anti-God human ways that include selfishness, pride, despair, superficiality, and lack of forgiveness.

We have seen that the evidence and the signs of a God worthy of worship come with a divine redemptive purpose and that this purpose can be sharply at odds with our own purposes. Accordingly, we easily can misunderstand the signs, if we notice them at all. The signs are intended by God to have humans join in full cooperation with God's redemptive goals, as the cases of Jonah and Jesus illustrate. Humans need to discern the divine love involved in the signs and to receive and appropriate it as the authoritative life-giving divine power it is.

In Paul's Good News message, humans appropriate the life-giving power of the signs when they willingly yield to (cooperate with) God's self-giving love on offer (manifested perfectly in Jesus) and become, by God's power, a "new creation." This new creation announced by Paul is no mere human belief or construct. It powerfully involves the moral and spiritual resurrection and reorientation of a willing person by God, as Paul witnessed firsthand (see Rom. 6:4–11; cf. Moser 2008, pp. 187–189).

The new creation has a key cognitive component. Accordingly, Paul remarks that "neither circumcision nor uncircumcision is anything; but a new creation is everything" (Gal. 6:15). In the same vein: "From now on, therefore, we regard no one from a human point of view; even though we once knew Christ from a human point of view, we know him no longer in that way. Therefore, if anyone is in Christ, there is a new creation" (2 Cor. 5:16–17; cf. John 3:1–14). Paul (aka Saul) had been a zealous persecutor of the followers of Jesus Christ (see Gal. 1:13–24), but in the presence of God's call through Jesus he came to acknowledge that Jesus is a living redemptive sign from God. He came to see someone formerly subject to his persecution as a sacred, life-giving sign from God.

When humans honestly face God's primary sign in Jesus Christ they also face the corresponding question from Jesus himself: "Who do you say that I am?" (Mark 8:29). This is an important example of divine corrective inquiry. One's answer can affect not only one's perception of evidence for God but also one's future regarding one's being in or out of companionship with God. Not all alleged miracles are genuinely of God, of course, but the sign of Jesus Christ himself, as a personal agent, satisfies the criterion of divine self-giving love and calls us to enter life in companionship with God. Entering such a life will take one beyond mere reflections and arguments; it will lead to volitional cooperation and companionship with a supernatural agent famous for human deliverance and renewal via divine corrective reciprocity.

Although deep deliverance by God is rigorous owing to many human anti-God tendencies, it begins to make us morally new, in reverent companionship with God. This is moral and spiritual *re-creation* by the God of *agapē*. When we follow Jesus Christ in Gethsemane, we apprehend God's unmatched *power* of *agapē* (no mere talk), and we begin to appreciate the following wisdom from Chesterton (1927):

> After one moment when I bowed my head
> And the whole world turned over and came upright,
> And I came out where the old road shone white,
> I walked the ways and heard what all men said,
> Forests of tongues, like autumn leaves unshed,
> Being not unlovable but strange and light;
> Old riddles and new creeds, not in despite
> But softly, as men smile about the dead.
> The sages have a hundred maps to give
> That trace their crawling cosmos like a tree,
> They rattle reason out through many a sieve
> That stores the sand and lets the gold go free:
> And all these things are less than dust to me
> Because my name is Lazarus and I live.

What of philosophy in the wake of such divine re-creation? Must it cease altogether? No, if the philosophy in question is open, at least in principle, to *de re* volitional engagement with God. (Not all philosophy, however, is open in this way; philosophy can be stubbornly narrow in excluding the severe God who intervenes for the sake of the redemption of humans.) Philosophy done under divine authority differs from philosophy not done under such authority. A big difference is in the purpose of doing philosophy and the resulting focus. Philosophy done under divine authority includes redemptive Good News urgently needed by humans, and philosophers should be faithful to this Good News as they experience it. (Chapter 5 outlines this story.)

Postponing the Good News message for the sake of supposed philosophical preliminaries often leaves philosophers languishing indefinitely in such preliminaries. We see this when philosophers of religion never get around to honest reflection on the vital existential and moral struggle that is human faith in God. Perhaps we do not need to languish there, after all. At least, that is what this chapter contends, in its use of Gethsemane to redirect epistemology regarding God's reality. We now need to look a bit more carefully at the kind of re-creation on offer, in the light of the severity of God.

CHAPTER FOUR

Severity and salvation

> Work out your own salvation with fear and trembling; for it is
> God who is at work in you, enabling you both to will and to
> work for his good pleasure.
>
> (Phil. 2:12–13)

> It is the Spirit who gives life. Yes, the Spirit gives life – through
> death.
>
> (Kierkegaard 1851a, p. 77)

Soteriology, or the explanation of salvation, includes the distinctive Christian approach to salvation developed by the apostle Paul.
We shall see that Paul's gospel of salvation does not fit with many
influential modern interpretations, but that it is nonetheless resilient and powerful, in keeping with the severity of God. According
to this chapter, Paul's case for salvation by divine "grace" requires
an active, if severe, role for humans in their salvation. In identifying this active role, we shall elucidate our own accountability in
the realization of human salvation. The chapter clarifies this active
role via an important distinction between (a) action that either *constitutes* or *earns* salvation and (b) action that *receives* already constituted salvation. The chapter illuminates the nature of divinely
reckoned righteousness in terms of human faith that is rigorously
active concerning (b) but not (a) in the salvation that involves the
human reception of divine resurrection power.

GRACE AND WORKS

Paul's account of salvation is theocentric in that it revolves around a distinctive perspective on *God*. He announces: "the gospel … is the power (*dunamis*) of God for salvation (*sōtērian*) to everyone who has faith … for in it the righteousness (*dikaiosunē*) of God is revealed" (Rom. 1:16–17). The Christological emphasis of Paul's soteriology stems from its *theo*centric character, and not vice versa; that is, Paul's Christology owes its importance to God's redemptive plan in Christ. His soteriology highlights God's righteousness, which concerns God's powerful life-giving moral character and redemptive purposes and figures directly in Paul's understanding of human salvation via God's grace in the death and resurrection of Jesus Christ.

Paul portrays God as having undertaken a powerful salvific mission whereby God "puts forward" Jesus in his death and resurrection as a life-giving means of dealing with human alienation from God and its resulting death (Rom. 3:25, 4:24–25, 6:23). More specifically, the divine aim here, according to Paul, is to show that in dealing with human alienation God is both righteous (*dikaios*) and the one who justifies (*dikaiounta*), and thereby saves, the person with a certain kind of receptive human faith in God (Rom. 3:26).

Paul thinks of God's justifying activity through human faith as including God's justifying the ungodly person (*asebē*) and thereby giving lasting life to that person in companionship with God (Rom. 4:5, 5:6, 17–18). One might have assumed that God would justify only the self-made righteous person, but this is not Paul's view. His soteriology offers a surprise here, but the surprise aims to preserve God's distinctive righteousness while portraying God as mercifully salvific toward receptive humans. After all, this God, represented by Jesus prior to Paul, is famous for loving God's enemies.

God's gambit, according to Paul, is to provide salvation to humans by not crediting, or reckoning (*logisētai*), their sin to them, while maintaining and offering divine righteousness via God's role in the death and resurrection of Jesus. Paul finds the idea of God's not reckoning sin to sinful humans in the Psalms (32:1–2, LXX version; cf. Rom. 4:8). He also finds the idea of God's reckoning righteousness to the ungodly, apart from human merit, in the Genesis story of Abraham (Gen. 15:6, LXX version; cf. Rom. 4:3). This divine reckoning of righteousness, including not reckoning sin, must avoid making God's gambit a legal fiction, including a false attribution to ungodly humans. It can do this if it involves not just an acquittal as forgiveness but also a certain kind of change toward righteousness in a human recipient. We shall see how to avoid such a fiction and thereby to identify the heart of Paul's redemptive message.

In Paul's soteriology, God promises and delivers a kind of righteousness to humans that "leads to … life for all" concerned (Rom. 5:18; cf. Rom. 4:16). In addition, Paul claims that God intends divine grace to "reign through righteousness" in a way that leads to lasting human life through Jesus Christ (Rom. 5:21, RSV). Keeping divine mercy and righteousness together, this God "gives life to the dead and calls into existence the things that do not exist" (Rom. 4:17). Paul suggests that, unlike God, a moral law cannot yield the needed righteousness, because a moral law by itself cannot give life to people, whereas righteousness requires life (Gal. 3:21). Paul's driving assumption is that God seeks to give life to humans and uses means that serve that purpose (at least so far as humans cooperate). The divine redemption of humans, accordingly, is God's giving lasting life with God to cooperative humans.

The God of Abraham, according to Paul, promises a lasting life that includes the human inheritance of the world (Rom. 4:13). In contrast, a morally robust law, such as the Mosaic law, will call only for deserved wrath, instead of life, owing to human failure to keep it perfectly (Rom. 4:15; cf. Rom. 3:9, 19–20, 23). Paul assumes, then, that the righteousness needed by humans must be life-giving and thus powerful toward human salvation as life (in cooperation) with God (cf. Rom. 1:16–17), and that only God can fill the order for such power. A key issue concerns *how* God fills this tall order while remaining righteous in the salvation of unrighteous humans. Paul assumes that humans cannot achieve, earn, or otherwise secure life on their own and therefore cannot possess life-giving righteousness or salvation on their own. They need outside help in this regard, and this should come as no surprise if the standard is the morally perfect character of a God worthy of worship.

Paul identifies a means of righteousness that does not depend on a law leading to human failure and condemnation. The *means* in question is not a *source* of righteousness, but it preserves God's unique status as righteous and life-giving and conveys something of this status to unrighteous recipients. In keeping with the story of Abraham in Genesis 15, the means is human faith (*pistis*) in God and thus is not the moral law or the Mosaic law (Rom. 4:13). Faith in God is crucial, according to Paul, because it enables God's promise to Abraham of lasting life and inheritance of the world to rest on a gift of divine "grace" (*charis*) and to be available to all people, not just the physical descendants of Abraham (Rom. 4:16).

Paul understands divine grace in terms of a divine *gift*: "apart from law, the righteousness of God has been disclosed … [A]ll who believe … are now justified by his grace as a gift (*dōrean*), through the redemption that is in Christ Jesus" (Rom. 3:21–22, 24; cf. Rom. 5:15). (He uses the terms *charisma, dōrea,* and *dōrēma* equivalently for the "free gift" of grace, in Romans 5:15–17, 6:23.) Paul contrasts a gift of grace with works (*erga*) that involve satisfying a debt due to be paid: "Now to one who works (*ergazomenō*), wages are not

reckoned as a gift (*kata charin*) but as something due (*opheilēma*)"
(Rom. 4:4). This remark is central to understanding Paul's widely
misunderstood notion of human works that contrasts with his
notion of divine grace (but *not* with his idea of human action or
obedience).

Why, in the case of "one who works," are the wages reckoned
by God as a debt due to be paid? Is this divine reckoning actually a
fiction and thus arbitrary relative to the fact of the matter regarding
works? In that case, works would not genuinely involve a debt due
to be paid, contrary to Paul's characterization of the reckoning of
wages for works. This, however, would be an implausible position
that undermines Paul's claim about reckoning and works. Paul must
have in mind, then, a kind of working that involves one's aiming, if
implicitly, to satisfy a debt due to be paid by oneself. Otherwise, his
suggested connection between human works and divine reckoning
in terms of something due would be misguided and misleading.

Paul's notion of works here is *not* to be identified with the more
general notion of human *acts* or *deeds*, such as acts of obedience,
because not all such acts involve a debt due to be paid. Accordingly,
Paul can consistently say: "Circumcision is nothing, and uncircumcision is nothing, but obeying the commandments of God is everything" (1 Cor. 7:19). This is a difficult statement for interpreters who
make divine grace incompatible with human obedience. Paul also
can consistently understand a person's being led by God's Spirit and
being a child of God in terms of that person's action of putting to
death the deeds of one's sinful body by the power of God's Spirit
(Rom. 8:13–14).

Human "works" (as earnings) have no place in divine grace or
reckoned righteousness in Paul's soteriology. We should not infer,
however, that human *deeds* have no place in the human reception
of divine grace. It is still a live option, then, that human faith in

God involves human deeds in the human reception of divine grace. Human acting is not automatically human earning or even intended human earning. Accordingly, divine grace can require human acting, even human obeying, although such grace excludes the human earning of God's approval. A requirement of human earning of divine love would be at odds with the recurring theme in the New Testament, particularly in Paul and in John, that God *first* loved humans. It therefore would conflict with Paul's and John's understandings of divine grace.

Paul's contrast between grace and works is explicit: "if it [God's salvation of humans] is by grace, it is no longer on the basis of works (*ergōn*), otherwise grace would no longer be grace" (Rom. 11:6). (The translation of *ergōn* here by "deeds done" (NEB) or "deeds" (REB and Fitzmyer 1992) is seriously mistaken; the same is true of the KJV translation of *ergōn* as "deeds" in Rom. 3:20, 28.) Divine grace toward humans, according to Paul, excludes human works understood as involving one's satisfying a debt due to be paid to God and thereby earning God's approval. Grace as a divine gift of righteousness for a person is incompatible with works as involving that person's paying a debt either to constitute or to earn righteousness before God. This is a clear implication of Romans 4:4 and 11:6.

Contrary to some proponents of the "new perspective" on Paul (see, for instance, Dunn 1985; 1988, vol. I, p. 158; 1998, pp. 334–379), Paul's exclusion of human works from divine grace is not limited to deeds required by the law as national Jewish identity markers. Paul excludes from grace human works *of any sort* that involve a human's satisfying a debt due to be paid to God. His concern about works in Romans, then, is not restricted to Jewish identity markers. (For further support for this important correction to the "new perspective," see Cranfield 1991; Kim 2002, pp. 57–66; and Das 2009.)

Paul assumes that humans on their own, whether Jewish or Gentile, fall short of constituting or earning their righteousness before God (see Rom. 3:9, 19–20, 23). Accordingly, if God credits just on the basis of what humans constitute or earn, they will not be reckoned as righteous before God. Part of Paul's gospel, however, is that God has a different, gracious means of credit toward humans: human faith in God. He finds this message of good news anticipated in the Genesis story of Abraham as "the father of all of us," Jews and Gentiles alike (Rom. 4:16). We distort Paul if we focus his point on Jewish identity markers. He seeks a resolution of the human predicament in the face of God's redemption in Jesus Christ.

GRACE AND FAITH

Paul contends that "God reckons righteousness apart from works"; more specifically: "to one who without works trusts (*pisteuonti epi*) him who justifies the ungodly, such faith is reckoned as righteousness" (Rom. 4:5–6). Paul's talk of "such faith" here refers back to an active participle (*pisteuonti*, "trusts") that signifies a deed-involving human contribution to a situation where God reckons righteousness. This contribution is deed-involving because it involves a human's *doing* something, namely, *trusting* in God. It does not follow, of course, that such faith in God is *just* a human deed, because it also may involve state-like, dispositional features that go beyond mere deeds. Even so, Paul's use of an active participle indicates a deed-involving feature of human faith in God, and therefore such faith cannot be portrayed accurately apart from human activity (which differs from human earning).

If, contrary to our evidence, Paul identified "works" with human deeds, he would be claiming the following in Romans 4:5: to one who *without doing any deeds does the deed* of trusting him who justifies the ungodly, such faith is reckoned as righteousness. This, of course, would be logically incoherent, and we have no reason whatever to ascribe such obvious incoherence to Paul. Romans 4:5, then, should discourage any inclination to confuse Paul's notion of "works" with the notion of "human deeds." It should correct any distorted notion of divine grace that excludes human activity in the reception of such grace.

Human faith in God, in Paul's perspective, is the deed-involving medium for the human receiving of divine righteousness and grace. More specifically, it is the human deed-involving medium for reception of the divine reckoning, or crediting, of divine righteousness to willing humans (cf. Rom. 4:11, 16, 24). This medium involves humans actively and rigorously in their redemption by God in virtue of their active and rigorous reception of the divine righteousness offered as a free gift. Paul remarks about Abraham: "No distrust made him waver concerning the promise of God, but he grew strong (*enedunamōthē*) in his faith as he gave glory to God, being fully confident that God was able to do what he had promised. Therefore (*dio*) his faith 'was reckoned to him as righteousness'" (Rom. 4:20–22; see also Rom. 11:20 on how Gentiles "stand only through faith"). Paul stresses the active, intentional resolve of Abraham in response to God's promise as a crucial factor in the divine reckoning of righteousness to Abraham. Paul sees no conflict between such active human resolve and the realization of divine grace in humans.

The NRSV translation, "grew strong in his faith," in Romans 4:20 is inferior to the more literal translation that captures the passive voice of *enedunamōthē*, "was empowered in his faith." The latter translation suggests the view of Paul that *God* empowered Abraham through the latter's deed-involving faith in God. (See Phil. 4:13, where Paul uses the corresponding active participle, *endunamounti,* with reference to a divine source of the empowering of himself.) Accordingly, the more literal translation allows one to capture Paul's view of human faith in God as one's actively receiving, and thereby being empowered by, God's free gift of righteousness. Human faith in God is not humanly passive, in Paul's soteriology, and this is no threat at all to robust divine grace in the salvation of humans.

The available empowerment of a human by God through human faith can save Paul from advocating a legal fiction in the divine reckoning of righteousness to humans. In particular, the power of righteousness received as a divine gift through faith in God can inaugurate and sustain an actual process of change in a person toward being made righteous by God (cf. Rom. 5:19, 2 Cor. 5:21). God's reckoning of righteousness would not then be a legal fiction, given a corresponding actual change in receptive humans owing to God's redemptive power, even if the change is the initial stage of a larger, rigorous process of human maturation in divine righteousness. A beginning change is still a real change, despite the need for further change. So, the charge of a legal fiction would be misplaced.

According to Paul, divine righteousness and thus salvation for humans rest on grace as a divine gift, and such grace is incompatible with human works as either constituting or earning righteousness before God. In Paul's perspective, accordingly, the human faith in God that is the medium for divine righteousness must be free of human works as constituting or earning such righteousness. Paul contends that God redeems, or saves, humans by a gift of divine grace reckoned through faith in God rather than by any human constituting or earning of divine approval. As the core of Paul's gospel of grace, this view precludes the *constituting* or *earning* of righteousness before God by human activity, but it nonetheless allows for an active human role, via human faith and even obedience, in the human *receiving* of such righteousness. Although humans are not active in constituting or earning the righteousness being offered to them, they still can be active in the reception of such righteousness.

There can be human *receptive actions*, such as trusting in God, that do not involve any human intention to constitute or to earn a status before God. This is the conceptual key to putting together the pieces of Paul's otherwise puzzling remarks on grace, faith, and works. This key makes some sense of divine severity in God's demanding rigorous human activity in the reception of divine grace. The rigorous human activity can be an important, properly challenging factor in the transformation of humans toward God's moral character of righteousness.

Paul contrasts faith and works as follows:

Gentiles, who did not strive (*diōkonta*) for righteousness, have attained it, that is, righteousness through faith; but Israel, who did strive for the righteousness that is based on the law, did not succeed in fulfilling that law. Why not? Because they did not strive for it on the basis of faith (*ek pisteōs*), but as if it were based on works. (Rom. 9:30–32)

Regarding Israel, Paul adds: "being ignorant of the righteousness that comes from God (*tou theou*), and seeking to establish (*stēsai*) their own (*idian*), they have not submitted to God's righteousness (*tou theou*)" (Rom. 10:3). Accordingly, Paul distinguishes between two kinds of righteousness: (a) the righteousness "from God," by way of a divine gift of grace, and (b) the righteousness humans seek to establish, by way of their own works, to pay a debt and thus to constitute or to earn their good standing with God.

Paul suggests that alternative (b) involves a self-destructive human failure to submit to the righteousness from God by grace through faith in God. Paul's talk of "seeking to establish their own righteousness" should be understood in terms of humans seeking, via "works," either to constitute or to earn their approved status with God. The latter seeking, in Paul's soteriology, is a human disaster, because it disregards God's life-giving grace and righteousness. It is a sure path away from human salvation *by God*, the only salvation on offer according to Paul. Accordingly, it will not meet the standard of God's morally perfect character.

Israel's pursuit of righteousness, according to Paul, was not based on faith in God but instead was "as if it were based on works" of the law. Following his outlined autobiography as "a member of the people of Israel" (Phil. 3:5), Paul avows pursuit "not [of] a righteousness of my own (*emēn*) that comes from the law, but ... [of] the righteousness from God (*ek theou*) based on faith" in God (Phil. 3:9). Paul is *not* accusing all of the other Jews before him or contemporaneous with him as seeking to constitute or to earn righteousness before God via the law. Instead, he is identifying this tendency in his own earlier life as a law-observant Jew who was "as to righteousness under the law, blameless" (Phil. 3:6). (The relevant kind of blamelessness does not entail moral perfection before God.)

Paul assumes that he is not alone in a tendency toward self-righteousness, but this is no denunciation of either Judaism properly understood or of all (or even most) other Jews as seeking righteousness via human earning. Under the lordship of Christ, Paul had come to count his "gain" of blamelessness relative to the law as "loss" for the sake of having the righteousness from divine grace (or, an unearned gift) through faith in God (Phil. 3:7–9). The latter righteousness comes as a divine gift and therefore leaves no room to be either constituted or earned via human works of the law.

Paul's talk of "works" (*erga*), like his talk of "law" (see Rom. 8:2), takes on different meanings in different contexts in his letters. Accordingly, one cannot plausibly hold that whenever Paul uses "works" or "work" he has in mind the paying of a debt that is due. The aforementioned sense of "works" as involving the human paying of a debt cannot be generalized, then, to all occurrences of Paul's use of *erga*. For instance, he talks without restriction of the "work of faith" (*ergou tēs pisteōs*) in 1 Thessalonians 1:3 and of the "work of God" (*ergon tou theou*) in Romans 14:20. Neither of these contexts concerns the human constituting or earning of a status before God. Paul's language, then, resists sweeping generalizations and calls for careful attention to the relevant linguistic contexts. Attention to this lesson will encourage a resilient perspective on Paul on divine grace.

FAITH AND ACTION

Many interpreters have neglected the role in Paul's soteriology of active human faith in God. Consequently, widespread misunderstanding has arisen regarding the role of human activity in Paul's soteriology. We need to avoid two extremes in the interpretation of Paul on salvation by grace through faith in God. One extreme deactivates human faith in God; the other reduces it to a simple act. Neither of these extremes properly accommodates the role of divine severity in human redemption, particularly the severity brought by God to humans as agents with action-based dispositions.

The first extreme denies that faith in God is human deed-involving, on the ground that such deed-involving faith would undermine divine grace by making human righteousness and salvation depend on a human work. This extreme emerges in many Reformed Protestant interpretations, and it is encouraged by the English translations of Paul's letter to the Romans (for instance, Rom. 3:20, 28, 11:6) in the KJV, NEB, the REB, and Fitzmyer (1992).

Herman Ridderbos comments on Paul:

There can be no doubt whatever that faith, however much it bears the character of obedience and submission to the divine redemptive will, nevertheless does not rest on the assent of man himself ... but on the renewing and re-creating power of divine grace. Were it otherwise, then the gospel would be a new law, and the whole problem of the impotence of the law would recur. (1975, p. 234)

Such reasoning rests on a serious confusion between (a) a law as a human means of constituting or earning righteousness before God and (b) a law as a commandment to receive divine righteousness by grace through human faith in God. Paul opposes law in sense (a), but not in sense (b); indeed, sense (b) fits with his talk of "the law of faith" (Rom. 3:27; cf. Rom. 3:31). Ridderbos, among many other interpreters, shows no awareness of the crucial distinction between sense (a) and sense (b). Neglect of this distinction, however, will obscure an interpretation of Paul on Abraham's faith, particularly Paul's emphasis on the need for humans to "follow the example of the faith that our ancestor Abraham had before he was circumcised" (Rom. 4:12). The human following of such an example includes a definite human *activity*, if anything does.

As indicated, Paul holds: "Circumcision is nothing, and uncircumcision is nothing; but obeying the commandments of God is everything" (1 Cor. 7:19; cf. Rom. 7:22, 8:4). Paul, then, has no qualms about the importance of obeying God's commandments. Instead, he objects to any portrayal of law, commandment, or obedience as a human means to constitute or to earn righteousness before God. Accordingly, Paul is willing to talk of "obeying the Good News" (*hupēkousan tō euangeliō*) and to use this talk interchangeably with talk of "believing" (*episteusen*) the Good News (Rom. 10:16–17; cf. 2 Thess. 1:8).

Paul freely talks of the need to "submit to God's righteousness," which comes "from God" through faith in God rather than from earning God's approval via works (Rom. 10:4; cf. Rom. 9:30–32, 10:3). This talk fits well with Paul's own portrait of his mission from God "to bring about the obedience of faith among all the Gentiles"

(Rom. 1:5; cf. Rom. 16:26). The Good News of God's redemption in Christ, according to Paul, includes a divine command to obey God's call to faith through Christ. Accordingly, we empty this Good News of its divine imperative if we omit the role of active human obedience in faith in God. It is deeply ironic that many interpreters of *Paul* make this mistake. Perhaps they are reading Paul through a theory of divine sovereignty at odds with Paul's understanding of God's redemption of humans.

Paul assumes that people receive freedom from slavery to sin via their becoming "obedient from the heart" (*hupēkousate ek kardias*) to the Good News teaching presented to them (Rom. 6:17). This is part of what I have called Paul's *kardiatheology* (see Moser 2010a, chap. 4), which anchors the divine salvation of humans in matters of the human heart, including one's volitional center. Accordingly, and contrary to what many interpreters suggest, Paul can talk of "obedience, which leads to righteousness" (*hupakoēs eis dikaiosunēn*) (Rom. 6:16). (Significantly, Paul uses directly parallel talk, in Romans 10:10, of one's "believing with the heart" that "leads to righteousness.") This clear talk by Paul undermines any interpretation that separates Paul's notion of faith from his notion of obedience. In this vein, Paul speaks of the failure of Israel relative to his message as a matter of Israel's "unbelief" and "disobedience" (Rom. 11:20, 23, 30).

Given Romans 4:4–5 and 11:6, Paul definitely would *not* endorse any talk of "works, which lead to righteousness." His talk of "obedience" in Romans 6:16, then, must not be confused with his talk of "works" that connotes humans' constituting or earning righteousness. Accordingly, Paul's notion of obedience here is not to be subsumed under his notion of works that involve humans' constituting or earning righteousness. As suggested, therefore, Paul can talk of "the obedience of faith" (*hupakoēn pisteōs*) (Rom. 1:5, 16:26) without contradicting his key remarks about "works" in Rom. 4:4–5, 11:6.

Benjamin Schliesser endorses the extreme Reformed perspective that excludes human activity from faith:

[Paul's] argumentation ... puts all emphasis on the *activitas dei*. God has taken the initiative, and he makes the decisions. Therefore, for Paul faith is not the subjective condition for the event of salvation ... The radical opposition of faith and works in Paul ... renders inadequate all attempts that seek to retain the deed-character of faith. (2007, pp. 396–397)

Clearly, Schliesser conflates the notions of "works" and "human deeds," thus making the same mistake as the NEB and REB translations of Romans 11:6 and the KJV translation of Romans 3:20, 28. Paul does offer a "radical opposition" between faith and works (as seen in Romans 4:4–5 and 11:6), but it does not follow that he offers such an opposition between faith and *human deeds* or *actions*.

Paul frequently uses active verbs and participles to indicate the kind of human trusting crucial to the Abraham-like faith reckoned as righteousness by God (see, for instance, Rom. 3:22; 4:3, 5, 11, 17, 18, 21, 24; 6:17; 10:11–14, 16; 11:23; Gal. 2:16; 3:6). Paul would not have used such active verbal terms of humans if he did not have in mind human actions, which do not necessarily fall under his category of "works" in Romans 4:4–5. Accordingly, Paul does not "put all emphasis on the *activitas dei*." Schliesser's claim emerges from an extreme Reformed theology rather than from Paul's own writings, and that theology does not fit with Paul's perspective on divine grace through human faith in God.

Paul's acknowledged role for human activity in faith in God avoids any suggestion of faith as meritorious in virtue of humans' constituting or earning righteousness before God. In contrast, consider 1 Maccabees 2:52: "Was not Abraham found faithful when tested, and it was reckoned to him as righteousness?" This rhetorical question seems to recommend meritorious human faith, rather than the human reception of unearned righteousness. In Paul's contrary portrait, a person's being receptive of righteousness via faith in God does not entail that person's being *found worthy* by God of the status of righteousness. In Paul's portrait, God justifies the *un*godly (Rom. 4:5), and this is central to Paul's Good News. Receptively active faith, then, is not faithful action that merits righteousness before God. This neglected distinction goes a long way toward making good sense of Paul on divine grace through faith in God.

Ernest Best runs afoul of our distinction as follows:

The Jew understood *faith* in Gen. 15:6 as a definite activity on *Abraham's* part – his faithfulness to God's will; it was thus viewed as a form of *righteousness* which Abraham achieved, and Abraham was regarded as measuring up to God's standard – he was "justified by" something "he had done" (Rom. 4:2). (1967, p. 47)

Aside from the misleading monolithic talk of "the Jew," Best misses the key point that "a definite activity" need not be a "work" at all in Paul's sense in Romans 4:4–5. Paul holds that Abraham's faith includes "a definite activity" of trusting God (Rom. 4:3), but he denies that this receptive act constitutes or earns righteousness before God (Rom. 4:2–5).

As Best notes, Paul's notion of God's reckoning righteousness "does not mean 'reckoned as an equivalent' but indicates a *favour* on God's part: that God counts Abraham righteous is an act of his 'free grace alone' (3:24), and not a reward for Abraham's faith" (1967, p. 47; likewise, see Cranfield 1975, vol. I, p. 231). We now see, however, that such grace allows for and even demands receptive human action, such as human trust in God, by its recipients, and that such action differs from what Paul regards as "works" in Romans 4:4–5.

Stephen Westerholm offers a Reformed view of divine sovereignty that eclipses a human contribution to salvation, despite his effort to retain talk of a "human response" to God. On his reading of Paul, "humans can contribute *nothing* to their salvation" (2004, p. 351; cf.

p. 384). The problem with the law, according to Westerholm, is that it "demands deeds" and this "stands in contrast with God's grace" (2004, p. 311). This extreme portrait of Paul on grace contradicts the more modest approach under development here.

Westerholm's excluding the relevance of human deeds (and not just "works") does not fit with his characterization of faith as a "human response" (2004, p. 365). He remarks, "Paul is saying that the deeds of sinners cannot make them righteous, though God will declare them so if they credit and accept his offer of righteousness in Christ Jesus" (2004, p. 376). Such *accepting* is a human action and is therefore a human contribution to salvation, contrary to Westerholm's suggestion that "humans can contribute *nothing* to their salvation." Westerholm's approach thus leaves us with an inconsistency. The only plausible way to avoid inconsistency here is to distinguish (a) human receptive action as a component of faith in God and (b) human action that constitutes or earns righteousness before God. Action (a) is, however, a receptive contribution of humans to their salvation, and therefore Westerholm's approach cannot be sustained. (A similar problem undermines the Reformed approach of Campbell [2009, pp. 78–79, 829].)

The first interpretive extreme, as suggested, neglects the role in Paul's soteriology of humanly active faith in God. It thus misrepresents Paul's portrait of salvation by divine grace through humanly active, receptive faith in God. The result is a serious misunderstanding of the key role of human agency and thus of human responsibility, in Paul's soteriology. On this extreme, God's causal role in reckoning righteousness extinguishes human activity and accountability in the reception of salvation. This extreme position therefore empties a role for God's use of severity in human life to prompt humans to resolve, without coercion, to adopt or deepen faith in God.

The second extreme treats faith as a simple act, reducible to an episode of human action. Ernst Käsemann offers an approach to Pauline faith that maintains a crucial role for human activity. He remarks: "Faith is … the 'condition' of salvation, not as a human achievement, but as receiving and keeping the word which separates us from all lords and all salvation outside Christ" (1980, p. 109). He adds: "We must insist strongly that faith in Paul … is the act and decision of the individual person" (1980, p. 109). According to Käsemann: "Faith is not in itself righteousness … It is a condition as poverty is, or waiting for blessing" (1980, p. 111). He portrays the active receptivity of faith as allowing God's Word to be spoken to us and daring to live by it: "God comes to us in his promise and makes us righteous – righteous in that we, as the receivers, allow him to come to us" (1971, p. 93).

The views of Rudolf Bultmann underlie Käsemann's approach. Bultmann proposes that Paul understands *work* "in the fundamental sense – to earn claim to a reward." He contends that on Paul's view "faith, as decision, is even preeminently the deed of man," and he notes that "deeds" and "works" must be distinguished in Paul (1951, pp. 283–284). The deed of faith, Bultmann proposes, is a human act of self-surrender to the divine act of grace whereby one receives a new understanding of oneself that excludes human boasting before God (1951, pp. 300–301).

According to Bultmann, Paul's Good News "is, by nature, personal address which accosts each individual, throwing the person himself into question by rendering his self-understanding problematic, and demanding a decision of him" (1951, p. 307). This decision of faith "is a deed in the true sense: In a true deed the doer himself is inseparable from it, while in a 'work' he stands side by side with what he does" (Bultmann 1951, p. 316). Bultmann contrasts the deed of faith with human *accomplishment* by portraying it as obedient submission to God's way of salvation.

Bultmann and Käsemann acknowledge a crucial role for human activity in the realization of salvation among humans. They see that Paul regards the divine reckoning of righteousness as depending on human receptive activity toward God's redemptive call to humans. They also see that Paul portrays Abraham as responding to God with a kind of active faith in God that is a factor in God's reckoning righteousness to him (see Rom. 4:22). They thus acknowledge a definite human contribution, even if a purely active receptive contribution, to the realization of divine reckoned righteousness and salvation among humans.

While correcting the Reformed view, Bultmann and Käsemann go to a misleading extreme in portraying faith as *just* a human deed or act. They overlook that faith in God is not simply episodic in the way that a deed or an action is. A deed or an action is episodic in existing *only* while being performed. Faith or belief in God is not thus episodic, because it can exist even when a believer is not performing any actions, such as when fast asleep. One does not cease to have faith in God by, for instance, taking an action-free nap.

Faith in God requires a basis in the deed of one's trusting God at a time, but this deed need not be a constant episode in one's life. Faith in God is, accordingly, an action-based dispositional *state* whereby one has performed the deed of trusting God and, on that basis, would exercise (as an action) trust in God again in suitable circumstances. We do not need to identify here the exact circumstances (the relevant concept of faith in God lacks mathematical precision), but we can see that such action-based faith is not reducible to an episodic deed. It requires the receptive action of trust but can endure as a dispositional state even when one is doing nothing at all. Human receptivity to God, then, need not be an ongoing human action; it can endure instead as an action-based state relative to God. This approach avoids the aforementioned extremes in understanding human faith in God.

As an action-based *dispositional* state, human faith in God can persist (that is, does not cease to exist) when inactive and therefore can face a severe redemptive test from God even when not active as an episode. This is important, because it allows faith in God to be a subject of divine testing for the sake of human improvement even when a person is at rest, doing nothing at all. As a result, one cannot avoid divine severity in the testing of one's faith in God simply by going inactive. We have no such easy escape from divine severity for the sake of redemption in human life. In addition, as *action-based*, human faith in God includes a decisive role for human agency and thus human responsibility in the face of divine severity. God can test a person's faith in God, in order to manifest whether it is akin to Abraham's saving faith, and this test can regard the person as accountable in virtue of a decisive role for human agency in faith in God. Accordingly, we can avoid the shortcomings of the two extremes in question.

RECEIVING POWER

We need the important distinction between (a) an active human role in the *receiving* of divine salvation by human faith in God and (b) an active human role in the *providing* of salvation. We have identified Paul's view, in favor of option (a) and against option (b), that humanly active, receptive faith is a means of being empowered by God to bring divine salvation to humans who trust in God (Rom. 4:20). As a means, human faith in God is not an ultimate source of divine power, but it can effectively relate humans to such power, via human receptivity to this power. Such receptivity is needed, because

God does not coerce the wills of humans to trust in God and thereby to receive divine redemption.

The key activity of human faith in God is a *voluntary cooperative response* to divine involvement of various sorts in one's life: a response of *presenting oneself* cooperatively to God, with trust, to *receive* God's life-giving power of resurrection from the dead (Rom. 6:13, 16). Such faith is an affirmative human response to God's call to be transformed from spiritual death to new life in companionship with God. As Paul remarks: "Faith comes from what is heard, and what is heard comes through the word of Christ [or, of God]" (Rom. 10:17). This "word" is a call to receive, and to live by, resurrection power from God: "Present yourselves to God as those who have been brought from death to life" (Rom. 6:13).

We should acknowledge the *active* response ("Present yourselves") to God's life-giving intervention in the lives of "those who have been brought from death to life." The letter to the Colossians echoes this theme of spiritual resurrection: "You were also raised with him [Christ] through faith in the power of God" (Col. 2:12; cf. 3:1). This power of God is realized in humans who thereby (that is, on the basis of this power) bear the fruit of God's Spirit in being guided by God's Spirit: namely, love (*agapē*), joy, peace, patience, kindness, generosity, faithfulness, gentleness, and self-control (Gal. 5:22, 25; cf. Rom. 5:3–5, 8:2–16). (On the relation of such power to evidence for God, see Moser 2008; 2010a, chap. 4.)

The human reception of salvation, via faith in God, appropriates divine resurrection power, but it is no casual task. On the contrary, it bears the hallmark of divine severity, because it requires dying with Christ to sin in order to realize divinely empowered resurrection life now (see Rom. 6:10–11, 2 Cor. 4:10–11, Phil. 3:10–11, Gal. 2:20; cf. Byrnes 2003; Savage 1996; Hoskyns and Davey 1981). This resurrection life is a "new creation," motivated by "faith operating through love (*agapē*)" (Gal. 5:6, 6:15). God alone supplies the life-giving power, but humans are called to receive it via active, even struggling faith in God and his resurrection power. Such faith in God receives the divine power that "kills" one's sinful deeds in order to make room for the resurrection power of divine *agapē* among humans. (On this struggle of faith in God and its epistemological significance, see Chapters 2 and 3; cf. Moser 2010b.)

The divine power of salvation is humanly personified in Jesus Christ (Rom. 3:24, 1 Cor. 1:30), whom Paul portrays as a source of divine grace, but not as a recipient in need of it (Rom. 1:7, 5:15). Being righteous in his full obedience to God (Rom. 5:18, 19, Phil. 2:8–9), Jesus can bring the power of divine salvation to ungodly people as God's mediator in whom they actively trust (Rom. 9:33, Gal. 2:16). Through the death and resurrection of Jesus, God aims to manifest righteous and merciful *agapē* to humans and to invite them into lasting cooperative life with God (Rom 6:23, 11:32).

Paul summarizes the lesson as follows, in connection with the death of Jesus: "God has destined us not for wrath but for obtaining salvation through our Lord Jesus Christ, who died for us, so that whether we are awake or asleep we may live with him" (1 Thess. 5:9–10; cf. Rom. 14:9). This kind of reconciled living with God, however rigorous for humans, is the heart of divine salvation for humans. It comes not as just a theory but as good news empowered by self-giving *agapē*. It is marked by divine corrective inquiry and reciprocity (as outlined in Chapter 3) and by a kind of volitional, Gethsemane union between God and humans (portrayed in Chapter 5). The outstanding question, now and always, is whether humans are willing to receive such reconciled living with God, in an active struggle of trusting a severely righteous God who saves only by grace through faith in God.

OVERCOMING IMPEDIMENTS

Because the divine salvation of humans requires the reconciled living of humans with God, that is, in cooperation with God, such salvation includes much more than either mere divine forgiveness of humans or endless human life courtesy of God. It includes God's vigorous effort to prompt humans, without divine coercion, to live in cooperation with God, in keeping with God's perfect moral character.

In Paul's language, divine salvation requires that humans be "led by the Spirit of God" (Rom. 8:14), and this requires single-mindedness and volitional cooperation toward God as well as the use of God's power to end one's own anti-God attitudes and actions (Rom. 8:21). This is a tall order, but it is required by God's being worthy of worship and hence perfectly loving toward other agents. God seeks what is morally and spiritually best for humans, and therefore the rigorous transformation of humans is needed. Human wills, however, can block the full realization of God's redemptive effort, even if God recruits severity to try to advance the redemption of humans. Such is the dangerous price of God's allowing for free, morally responsible agents.

As Chapter 1 indicated, Paul thinks of God as having subjected creation to futility for the sake of prompting humans to enter into a life of cooperation with God as their priority over all other sources of security (Rom. 8:20–21). He also puts this lesson in terms of the human need to die to all anti-God (including selfish) power in order to live cooperatively with God in God's life-giving, resurrection power (see 2 Cor. 4:7–11, Phil. 3:7–11, Rom. 6:13, 8:36–39, Col. 3:1–6). A similar theme emerges from the teaching of Jesus in the Gospels. John's Gospel, for instance, portrays Jesus as saying: "Very truly, I tell you, unless a grain of wheat falls into the earth and dies, it remains just a single grain; but it if dies, it bears much fruit. Those who love their life lose it, and those who hate their life in this world will keep it for eternal life" (John 12:24–25; cf. Mark 8:34–36, Luke 14:27, Matt. 10:38–39). Accordingly, the divine salvation of humans faces a sharp, severe conflict between familiar human life and God's morally perfect life. Human life must die into God's life, as humans appropriate God's unique power via rigorous struggle.

Impediments to the divine salvation of humans are legion, but we can identify some prominent examples and counter them. Jesus apparently told the parable of the sower to explain the lack of complete or at least immediate success in his redemptive ministry. He identified at least three kinds of impediment: first, God's message of redemption in Christ can be snatched away from a person's heart; second, a person can be rootless and fall away from God in the face of life's severity; and third, the relatively superficial cares of the world and the intrigue of wealth can choke God's redemptive message (see Mark 4:13–19, Matt. 13:18–22, Luke 8:11–14). In the first case, a person fails to hold on to the message of God's redemptive *agapē* as a priority; this person allows God's Good News to disappear from his or her life. In the second case, a person folds in the presence of life's severity and gives up on God's severe redemption in Christ. In the third case, a person elevates worldly success and wealth in a way that suffocates God's redemptive message and power.

The first kind of impediment involves one's failing to embrace properly God's invaluable message and power of redemptive *agapē*, and, as a result, the message and the power disappear from one's life. Such a failure to hold on to God's power can arise from various human shortcomings, but one is particularly noteworthy. We may call it "human distancing from divine *agapē*." H. R. Mackintosh explains:

It is because we are such strangers to sacrifice that God's sacrifice leaves us bewildered. It is because we love so little that His love is mysterious. We have never forgiven anybody at such a cost as his … It is our unlikeness to God that hangs as an obscuring screen impeding our view … And the one cure for that is just to let God's own Spirit of love … fill our hearts and clear our vision. As the lessons of love are mastered, we shall more and more have understanding of [God's] wonderful grace that gave Christ for [all people]. (1938b, p. 177)

Divine love, being perfectly unselfish, is self-sacrificial for the benefit of others, even for enemies of God.

Divine sacrificial love is rare if not altogether absent in our own, independent motives, and, accordingly, we do not acknowledge or embrace it as the rare, life-giving treasure it is. Mackintosh adds: "Sacrifices are not after all abolished by Christianity … They are living men and women, boys and girls – living when brought to God's altar, living *because* brought there in glad, eager self-surrender" (1931, p. 8; cf. Daly 2009). Undeniably, we often distance ourselves from such sacrificial love. It therefore disappears from our list of priorities and hence from our focal areas of existence. It is, we might say, "snatched away" from us by the evil around us and within us. The Good News fades and then disappears from our lives. Our redemption likewise recedes and vanishes.

The second kind of impediment comes from the severity in human life, and this severity can take various general forms, whether physical, psychological, spiritual, or social. The list of actual instances of human severity seems endless, even if we were to bracket outright moral evil. We may call the common response "despairing over the severity of human life." In this response, a person responds to severity in human life, perhaps in one's own life, by giving up on divine redemption, by despairing over God's eventual triumph relative to life's severity. This person deems life too severe for the presence of a redemptive God. A common human assumption is that such a God would prevent the occurrence of the kind of severity found in human life.

A big part of the second kind of impediment is human failure to see how divine redemption proceeds, particularly in connection with the cross of Christ. James S. Stewart explains:

The Cross [of Jesus Christ] was the problem of evil at its worst ... the most terrifying triumph of sheer, naked evil. And yet it was that ... very stuff of sin which God has chosen to be the vehicle of his mightiest act of love. It is there, where sin has confidently proclaimed its supreme and final victory, that God has achieved sin's uttermost defeat. That is why Christian faith takes its stand at the Cross, and will triumph there ...

When you have seen [the Cross of Christ] ... you have seen God taking the worst that earth could do, and out of it fashioning the best that Heaven could bestow. You have seen Him taking "the hour and power of darkness" and making it victoriously the hour and power of light. After that, there can be no situation too difficult for God to handle, no irreparable disaster, no crown of thorns that He can't twist into a crown of glory. (1969, pp. 213–214)

The cross of Christ is a paradigmatic case of how divine redemption works in the midst of life's severity, including its evil, and it generalizes to other cases of severity in human life. A failure to appreciate how divine redemption works within life's severity can lead to despair in the face of such severity. In fact, much human despair over life's severity and divine redemption apparently stems from such a failure.

As Chapter 2 indicated, a theodicy for evil or severity is not at hand for humans, if it requires a full explanation of the divine purposes for God's permitting evil or severity. In addition, we have no firm ground to expect to be able to have such a theodicy in our earthly lives, given our real cognitive limitations regarding God's specific purposes. Even so, a significant response is available, and it comes not as a full explanation but as God's redemptive involvement in the midst of evil and severity. Paul points to this kind of response as follows: "We know that all things work together for good for those who love God ... [Nothing] in all creation will be able to separate us from the love of God in Christ Jesus our Lord" (Rom. 8:28, 39). Such an anchor against life's severity comes from God's elusive redemptive presence (what Chapter 2 called "non-separation from God") rather than from a full explanation of evil or severity in human life.

We should not infer that God is the cause of all of the severity that leads to human despair. A better view emerges from a parable attributed to Jesus in Matthew's Gospel, the parable of the wheat and the weeds. A disciple asks: "Master, did you not sow good seed in your field? Where, then, did these weeds come from?" The Master replies: "An enemy has done this" (Matt. 13:28). This parable suggests a kind of severity, including evil severity, that is not to be attributed to God. Personal agents other than God can have a formative causal role in some of life's severity, including evil severity. At the same time, God can use life's severity to bring redemption to humans, as long as they cooperate with life with God, in keeping with God's morally perfect character and will.

The third kind of impediment to divine redemption comes from human superficiality whereby one's cares about worldly success and wealth take precedence over God and God's redemptive will. As suggested, Jesus remarked that "there is need of only one thing" in connection with single-minded human cooperation with God's redemptive message (Luke 10:42). The widespread problem of human superficiality relative to worldly success and wealth is widely recognized among humans, even if we lack an easy cure. This is not a merely cognitive, or intellectual, problem, because the relevant superficiality involves the human will. As a result, no merely cognitive response will give the needed cure. Something deeper is needed, and it is found in the divine–human interpersonal reality we have called "divine corrective reciprocity" (see Chapter 3).

A cooperatively obedient human response in such reciprocity can lead one out of the superficiality in question toward a new priority for life in God's perfect will.

In different ways, the impediments noted resist divine corrective reciprocity as a priority, as the "one thing needful" for humans. Let's say, for short, that they resist *Gethsemane priority* by failing to make God's perfect, redemptive will a priority in human life. Accordingly, these impediments lead to the problems identified by the parable of the sower: (a) human failure to embrace properly God's redemptive Good News; (b) human despair over life's severity and over God; and (c) human superficiality toward worldly success and wealth. Gethsemane priority toward these impediments finds God's redemptive involvement and power at the center of a robustly good, if severe, human life, in a way that resituates the impediments under God's corrective reciprocity. Such priority is no abstract philosophical principle but must be anchored in a distinctive kind of volitional, Gethsemane union with God (identified in Chapter 5). This calls for profound human struggle with an elusive, severely redemptive God who will not lose a human soul to save a human body.

The human struggle in question is for one to awaken cooperatively to God at increasing depths of profundity and *agapē*. This kind of awakening requires one's being *willing* to awaken to God and the priority of God's perfect moral character and will. A person thus willing must embrace Gethsemane priority in a manner that receives and welcomes divine corrective reciprocity. That is, one must allow God's convicting will in conscience and experience to correct one's own inferior will and thereby redirect one's life cooperatively toward God. This is the heart of human cooperation with God, and it is a key purpose of divine severity in human salvation. Given God's worthiness of worship and hence moral perfection, we should expect such divine severity in human life, and understand human salvation accordingly. In other words, we should expect God to be vigorous in seeking to save human persons and lives, beyond human bodies. The next chapter identifies the experiential core of such salvation (as a distinctive kind of union with God) and the corresponding kardiatheology and Christian philosophy.

CHAPTER FIVE

Severity and philosophy

> Among the mature we do speak wisdom, though it is not a wisdom of this age or of the rulers of this age, who are doomed to perish. But we speak God's wisdom, secret and hidden.
>
> (1 Cor. 2:6–7)

> The fact that Christ can and does breathe his life into us, taking the first step in this true miracle of a communication of spiritual life, is one aspect of the whole fact which the term "mystic" is chosen to indicate rather than the term "moral."
>
> (Mackintosh 1923, p. 113)

We might think of a philosophy as having a shape, a form, or an image given by its presumed ultimate authority regarding the good, the true, and the beautiful. A rationalist philosophy that has just pure reason as its ultimate authority might be said to have a purely rational form, and an empiricist philosophy that has just empirical experience as its ultimate authority might be said to have a purely empirical form. In addition, a philosophy that has just sound arguments as its ultimate authority can be said to have a purely argumentational form.

A distinctly Christian philosophy would be neither purely rational nor purely empirical nor purely argumentational in form. Instead, it would accommodate the subversive Christian message that the outcast Galilean "*Jesus* is Lord" (1 Cor. 12:3; see Acts 2:36). In its talk of "Lord" (*kurios*), this message assigns distinctive authority to

Jesus Christ, even the authority proper to God (see, for instance, Phil. 2:9–11). The claim that Jesus is Lord figures not only in who counts as a Christian (namely, the one for whom Jesus is Lord) but also in which philosophy counts as Christian (namely, the one for whom Jesus is Lord).

A philosophy can be theistic or deistic without being Christian, because it can acknowledge that "God" is authoritative without affirming that Jesus is Lord. We can generalize this point to academic disciplines outside philosophy, such as theology, psychology, sociology, and the natural sciences. This chapter's aim, however, will be to clarify "Christ-shaped" philosophy as a model for other disciplines that acknowledges the role of divine severity in wisdom and philosophy.

Christian philosophy is a distinctive kind of philosophy owing to the special role it assigns to God in Christ. Much of philosophy focuses on concepts, possibilities, necessities, propositions, analyses, and arguments. This can be helpful as far as it goes, but it typically omits what is the distinctive focus of Christian philosophy: the redemptive *power* of God in Christ, available in the severity of human experience and life. Such power, of course, is not mere talk or theory. Even philosophers of a Christian persuasion, however, tend to shy away from the role of divine power in their efforts toward Christian philosophy.

The power in question goes beyond philosophical wisdom to the causally powerful, intentional Spirit of God, who intervenes with a goal of divine corrective reciprocity (as identified in Chapter 3). As this chapter indicates, this Spirit's power yields a distinctive religious epistemology and even a special role for Christian spirituality in Christian philosophy. The chapter acknowledges a goal of union with God in Christ that shapes how Christian philosophy is to be done, and the result should reorient such philosophy in various ways. No longer can Christian philosophers do philosophy without being, themselves, under corrective and redemptive inquiry by God in Christ. This chapter takes its inspiration from Paul's profound approach to philosophy in his letter to the Colossians. Oddly, this approach has been largely ignored even by philosophers of a Christian persuasion. We need to correct this neglect particularly if we are to understand the extent of the severity of God.

PAUL AS PHILOSOPHER

Following Jesus as the founder of the Christian movement, the apostle Paul is the most profound advocate of a Christ-shaped philosophy. (On the deep influence of Jesus on Paul's influential perspective, see Wenham 1995, 2002.) We therefore should attend to Paul's insights on the wisdom and the Spirit of Christ. Christian philosophy, in his approach, depends on God's Spirit, and the Spirit in question is Christ-shaped, being the Spirit of Jesus Christ. This perspective calls for a pneumatic epistemology and a Christ-oriented approach to the kind of wisdom sought by many philosophers since the time of Socrates and Plato. Reflective humans need a philosophy to live by, not just to think by, and Paul points us in the right, Christward direction.

The Spirit of Christ leads to the volitional struggle of Gethsemane (particularly, to the struggling *Jesus* in Gethsemane, where Calvary was sealed in cooperation with God). In doing so, this Spirit promises to lead us, noncoercively, from death to resurrection life (as lasting, reverent companionship with God) in all areas of our lives, regardless of our distinctive backgrounds and areas of interest. This story is Good News for humans, but it rarely gets a serious hearing from philosophers or other theorists. We will correct this deficiency. A key lesson will be that Christ-shaped philosophy should be joined with Christ-formed *philosophers*. It would be odd indeed to propose that a Christian philosophy has little to do with the conditions for *being* a Christian.

Paul's Letter to the Colossians offers a striking portrait of Christ-shaped philosophy. To that end, it offers a firm warning: "See to it that no one takes you captive through philosophy … and not according to Christ" (Col. 2:8). We should attend to the contrast between philosophy and Christ. Philosophy outside the authority of Christ, according to Paul, is dangerous to human freedom and life. The alternative is philosophy under (the authority of) Christ, and this involves a distinctive kind of wisdom. If philosophy is the love and pursuit of wisdom, then *Christian* philosophy is the love and pursuit of wisdom under the authority of Christ, which calls for an ongoing union with Christ, including one's cooperatively belonging to God in Christ.

Paul illuminates wisdom under Christ. As Chapter 1 indicated, he prays that the Christians at Colossae be filled with "spiritual wisdom (*sophia pneumatikē*) and understanding, so that you may lead lives worthy of the Lord, fully pleasing to him, as you bear fruit in every good work and as you grow in the knowledge of God" (Col. 1:9–10). "Spiritual wisdom," in Paul's approach, is wisdom intentionally guided and empowered by the Spirit of Christ. It therefore yields "lives worthy of the Lord, fully pleasing to him." No merely theoretical or intellectual wisdom has the power to guide such lives intentionally, and thus Paul refers to *spiritual* wisdom, which amounts to *Spirit-empowered* and *Spirit-guided* wisdom.

The divine redemption of humans calls for an *intentional* guide or agent who leads and empowers receptive humans inwardly, in accordance with God's character, even when rules and arguments fall short. Philosophers may seek concepts, analyses, principles, and arguments, but God sends a personal, intentional agent in Christ to secure human redemption. Even when concepts, analyses, principles, and arguments are a helpful means to an end, they are not the end itself in a Christian philosophy. The personal agent Christ is that divinely appointed end. This fact yields a living standard from which one can assess various concepts, analyses, principles, and arguments.

Paul links spiritual wisdom to "the word of Christ," to gratitude, and even to "spiritual songs," as follows: "Let the word of Christ (*logos tou Christou*) dwell in you richly; teach and admonish one another in all wisdom; and with gratitude in your hearts sing psalms, hymns, and spiritual songs to God" (Col. 3:16). The wisdom in question, Paul suggests, is anchored in "the word of Christ" and prompts the kind of gratitude that overflows in spiritual songs to God. One must suspect, then, that Paul would find secular philosophy deficient owing to its neglect of the word of Christ and spiritual songs to God. In this perspective, hymnody could be a neglected litmus test for a robust philosophy pleasing to God, but we cannot digress.

Paul's talk of "the word of Christ" is talk of *God's* word of Christ, and Paul offers in his Letter to the Colossians a definite portrait of God's word. He reports that he has been commissioned by God to make God's word fully known. In particular, he identifies God's word with "the mystery that has been hidden throughout the ages ... but has now been revealed" (Col. 1:26). Paul speaks of "the riches of the glory of this mystery, which is *Christ in you*, the hope of glory" (Col. 1:27). This mystery prompts him to "teach everyone in all wisdom," in order to "present everyone mature (*teleios*) in Christ," being "rooted and built up in him" (Col. 1:28, 2:7). God's main mystery, according to Paul, "is Christ himself, in whom are hidden all the treasures of wisdom" (Col. 2:2–3). This inward Christ is alive and interactive with God's wisdom and power.

Paul offers a cosmic picture of Christ as God's end: God created all things *for* (*eis*) Christ (Col. 1:16), so that he, Christ, might be preeminent in everything (Col. 1:18). If Christ is to be preeminent in everything, then he should be preeminent in philosophy and in every other academic discipline, too. According to Paul, "in [Christ] the whole fullness (*plēroma*) of deity dwells bodily, and [the Colossian Christians] have come to fullness in him, who is the head of every ruler and authority" (Col. 2:9–10). Christ's authority, then, is second to none in Paul's position; it is God's authority.

In Paul's grand portrait, God wants "everyone [to be] mature (or, complete) in Christ." Accordingly, God wants everyone, even every philosopher and every other person, to yield reverently to the authority of Christ, and this is not a merely external or juridical authority. Instead, the authority seeking maturity in Christ aims for a mysterious *inward union* (or, *communion*) between the exalted Christ and the people yielding and belonging to him as Lord. This inward union stems from God's aim that all people become Christlike in moral and spiritual character, anchored in reverent companionship with God as Father. It thus demands that one be an intentional agent who freely appropriates the life-giving power of Christ as Lord. Let's examine this vital power and identify its severity in human life.

UNION IN DIVINE *AGAPĒ*

Paul identifies the Colossian Christians as having "clothed yourselves with the new self, which is being renewed in knowledge (*epignōsis*) according to the image (*eikōn*) of its creator" (Col. 3:10). They are "being renewed" in "the image" of God and hence of Christ, who himself is "the image (*eikōn*) of the invisible God" (Col. 1:15; cf. Phil. 2:6, 2 Cor. 4:4). The renewal of humans in the image of God in Christ is no purely external matter, in Paul's philosophy. On the contrary, it is personally inward owing to an inward *agent-power* (rather than a mere event-power), as follows: "I have been crucified with Christ; and it is no longer I who live, but it is Christ who lives *in* (*en*) me. And the life I now live in the flesh I live by faith in the Son of God, who loved me and gave himself for me" (Gal. 2:19–20; cf. Gal. 1:15–16).

The agent-inwardness of Christ fits with Paul's statement to the Galatian Christians that "I am again in the pain of childbirth until Christ is formed *in* (*en*) you" (Gal. 4:19; cf. Rom. 8:10). It also fits with Paul's pointed question to the Corinthian Christians: "Do you not realize that Jesus Christ is in (*en*) you? – unless, indeed, you fail to meet the test!" (2 Cor. 13:5). His earlier, closely related question to them was: "Do you not know that you are God's temple and that God's Spirit dwells in (*en*) you?" (1 Cor. 3:16; cf. 2 Cor. 6:16, Phil. 2:13, Ezek. 36:26–27). We will clarify "the test" for the inward power of Christ.

Christ lives in Paul, but Paul does not suggest that he himself becomes extinguished or depersonalized by Christ. On the contrary, he affirms that he himself lives by faith in Christ. If Christ's agent-inwardness extinguished or depersonalized Paul himself, then Paul would not be able to live by faith in Christ or to have any faith at all. The Christ–human union, then, does not obliterate human selfhood. It does not entail an *absorption mysticism* that dissolves personal distinctions, as do some strains of Buddhism. As a result, Paul does not, and would not, say, "I am Christ." Instead, he honors Christ as God's Son who created him, loved him, forgave him, and redeemed him with inward divine power. Accordingly, Paul's talk of "unity" or "being one" with Christ (1 Cor. 6:17) does not entail *numerical* unity or oneness (cf. Mackintosh 1912, p. 334).

The key feature of Paul's idea of "Christ in you" is the inward agent-power of Christ working, directly at the level of psychological and motivational human attitudes, toward a cooperative person's renewal in God's image as God's beloved child. We may call this appeal to the inward agent-power of Christ the *Gethsemane union* approach to "Christ in you." It is union with *God* in Christ, given that it is union with the perfect will of God in Christ.

An alternative view proposes that Christ–human union is merely ethical, in virtue of one's being committed to the authoritative ethical commands from Christ. In this view, a human and Christ are united just by their sharing ethical commitments toward God and others. Sometimes this view is expressed in terms of humans' sharing with Christ acceptance of the divine love-commands and their unifying power among humans. Christ, according to this view, gives divine love-commands, and Paul commits himself to them. As a result, Christ and Paul are ethically and volitionally united in virtue of their sharing these commands as commitments.

Paul's approach to human union with Christ resists a reduction to shared ethical commitments, even when divine love-commands are centrally present. Ethical commitments and commands do not yield the inward agent-power of Christ that is central to human union with Christ. Paul explains to the Corinthian Christians: "[Christ] is not weak in dealing with you, but is powerful in (*dunatei en*) you. For he was crucified in weakness, but lives by the power of God" (2 Cor. 13:3–4). No mere ethical or juridical account of union will capture the inward agent-power of Christ mentioned by Paul. One can have all of the right ethical or juridical commitments but lack the power of Christ to carry out those commitments.

The power in question corresponds to Paul's talk of a "test" of whether "Jesus Christ is in you" (2 Cor. 13:5). The test is for an inward agent-power characterized by Paul as follows: "hope [in God] does not disappoint us, because God's love (*agapē*) has been poured into (*en*) our hearts through the Holy Spirit that has been given to us" (Rom. 5:5; cf. 2 Cor. 4:6). As Chapter 3 suggested, Paul would say that *faith in God* does not disappoint us either but passes the test for the same reason: we have been flooded in our deepest experience by the presence and power of God's personal *agapē*, courtesy of the Spirit of Christ. Without this actual experience, one will have a hard time adequately understanding the Good News of God in Christ.

An appeal to the testimony, or the witness, of God's Spirit will fall short, cognitively and existentially, if it omits reference to the humanly experienced flood of *agapē* from God's Spirit. It then will be too remote from God's actual, self-revealed moral character in Christ and hence will be too amorphous to represent the severely redemptive God. Christian philosophy should hallmark this unique vital flood in its epistemology of God (as Chapter 3 suggested).

Faith in God is neither mere assent to a proposition ("even the demons believe") nor a leap in the dark (see Chapters 3 and 4). Instead, it is the *responsive* cooperative commitment of oneself to the God who sends his Spirit with *agapē* and forgiveness for the sake of Gethsemane union with Christ. Faith in God includes one's ongoing resolve to receive God's moral character in Christ inwardly and to belong to God, in the reverent attitude of Gethsemane. God calls first by showing us his *agapē* for us, and human faith responds with receptive, cooperative self-commitment to this God who intervenes in our experience. When we remove the needed human resolve from faith in God, we end up with faith that lacks a vital human struggle to make Christ preeminent in our moral characters and lives. We then have dead faith, however much philosophy and theism we have.

Amazingly, divine love comes to God's *enemies*, including us (Rom. 5:6, 10, Col. 1:21), and therefore we can test for God's love in us by testing for inward love and forgiveness of our enemies, including our intellectual enemies. To the extent that we resist inward enemy-love, we resist God himself, however shrewd our arguments and theories for theism. To that extent, we also resist God's aim that "the love from Christ urge us on," even toward forgiving and blessing our enemies (2 Cor. 5:14). Painfully, but helpfully, there is nothing abstract or amorphous about this test for the inward Christ and his salient power; in other words, this test has sharp, severe teeth. As a result, we often prefer to ignore such a test for God's disturbing presence. Minimal honesty in the teeth of this test reveals our desperate need for divine grace and renewal in the image of Christ as God's beloved children.

Paul puts his point about God's redemptive life in terms of the "Spirit of Christ" as follows:

You are in the Spirit, since the Spirit of God dwells in (*en*) you. Anyone who does not have the Spirit of Christ does not belong to him. But if Christ is in (*en*) you, though the body is dead because of sin, the Spirit is life [for you] because of righteousness. (Rom. 8:9–10)

Paul comes very close to using "the Spirit of God" and "the Spirit of Christ" interchangeably, and he suggests that having the Spirit of Christ in you is virtually the same as "Christ … in (*en*) you." We need not try to specify the metaphysical relations underlying his position; instead, we shall identify some functional features of the union in question.

Paul identifies an inward agent testifying, or bearing witness, to God's redemptive love: "When we cry [or shout], 'Abba! Father!,' it is that very Spirit [of God] bearing witness with our spirit that we are children of God" (Rom. 8:15–16; cf. Gal. 4:6, 2 Cor. 1:22, 5:5). God's testifying Spirit thus can be loud at times, and therefore we should hesitate to try to reduce the relevant testimony to Calvin's "*secret* testimony of the Spirit" (*Institutes* 1, vii. 4). (For some relevant exegetical discussion, see Dunn 1998, pp. 419–434.)

Paul is well aware of false spirits that oppose the Spirit of God, and therefore he gives real specificity to his approach, beyond vague talk of a divine "spirit." He gives form or shape *de re* to his Spirit talk by means of the *life*, including the inward life, of the crucified and risen Christ, not just by means of *de dicto talk* about his life. The actual *de re* life of Christ differs from *de dicto* talk about this life, because the former has a distinctive *agent-power* not possessed by the latter. (Christ is a personal agent with intentional power, including the power of *agapē* and forgiveness; talk is not.) The agent-power in question stems from the inward life of Christ (who, Paul says, intentionally loved him and forgave him), and it shapes how God's Spirit witnesses to God's reality, love, forgiveness, and faithfulness.

The agent-power of divine *agapē* in Christ enables the afore-mentioned kind of witness mentioned in Romans 5:5; that is, God's love (*agapē*) poured out in (*en*) our hearts. This is God's self-giving love for his children, including for Jesus as God's pre-eminent son. Such humanly experienced *agapē* prompts the filial cry immortalized by Jesus and his earliest followers, "Abba! Father!" Accordingly, the witness of God's Spirit with our spirit is based on agent-*power*, anchored in God's flooding a receptive human heart with his distinctive love of the kind shown in his preeminent agent, Christ. This life-changing power and the corresponding test for it go beyond mere truth, knowledge, understanding, or explanation. They involve powerful *agapē* that is inherently person-oriented, as an agent-power, and resists a reduction to anything nonpersonal. Such *agapē* can be found, for instance, in cases where humans genuinely care for their resolute enemies.

One can receive God's power of *agapē* even if one has a very limited understanding or explanation of it. In addition, Paul puts this agent-power first in his list of the fruit of God's Spirit in humans (Gal. 5:22), and he exalts this power above mere faith, hope, knowledge, prophecy, and self-discipline (1 Cor. 13; cf. 1 Cor. 8:1). Prior to Paul, Jesus himself had indicated that the power of *agapē* underwrites being his disciple under "Abba, Father," and being known as such a disciple (see Matt. 5:43–48, John 13:35). His test was this distinctive agent-power from God.

Paul thinks of the power of *agapē* within receptive humans as the power of the inward Christ, the living intentional Christ within such humans. Accordingly, this power is no mere virtue, principle, argument, or human commitment. The power in question conforms to and sustains the pattern of the life of Christ. Paul writes: "I want to know Christ and the power of his resurrection and the sharing of his sufferings by becoming like him in his death, if somehow I may attain the resurrection of the dead" (Phil. 3:10–11). Similarly, he remarks: "While we live, we are always being given up to death for Jesus' sake, so that the life of Jesus may be made visible in our mortal flesh" (2 Cor. 4:10–11). We are to live out in our own lives, over time, the pattern of the self-giving life of Christ, who empowers us with divine *agapē* from within, as long as we are receptive and cooperative. If we have been united (*sumphutoi*) with Christ in his death, according to Paul, we are to live now in the newness of life with the risen Christ (Rom. 6:4, 5, 11, 13; cf. Col. 3:1).

Moving toward God's severity, Paul characterizes divine *agapē* as cruciform, as moved by and conformed to the divine motive that led to the cross of Jesus. He urges the Philippian Christians to have "the same mind in you that was in Christ Jesus … who humbled himself and became obedient to the point of death – even death on a cross" (Phil. 2:5, 8). This calls for cooperation with "the God who is at work in (*en*) you, enabling you both to will and to work for his good pleasure" (Phil. 2:13). Such non-coerced cooperation, like the corresponding Gethsemane union, is redemptively severe; it calls for dying to all anti-God ways in order to live into God's morally perfect life as a priority. This rigorous struggle, according to Paul, is a matter of "work[ing] out your salvation with fear and trembling" (Phil. 2:12), which (as Chapter 4 noted) is not a matter of working to earn salvation from God. The struggle rigorously seeks to appropriate the redemptive power of God's unearned grace, and then to manifest (and offer) it for the sake of others.

Christ's self-giving obedience to God, according to Paul, shows God's distinctive love for humans: "God proves his love for us in that while we still were sinners Christ died for us" (Rom. 5:8). This death manifests the faithful obedience represented in Gethsemane, where Jesus cried "Abba! Father!" and then obeyed God with everything he had (Mark 14:36). He humbled himself, obediently and reverently, in yielding his will and his life to God's perfect will. This is the personal, human paradigm of Gethsemane union with God. Above all else, it is what God seeks in the redemption of humans, for the good of humans.

Even if the death of Christ is "for us," as many Christians rightly emphasize, we should ask how this event becomes powerful *to us, in the pattern of our lives*. Christ's death is, of course, an event of ancient history, roughly dateable to a Friday in April of AD 33. One could propose that its power is only that of a historically remote event, inadequately powerful to make a contemporary life new and resilient with divine *agapē*, in companionship with God. Clearly, however, the historical cross of Christ must not be left as *merely* historical, if it is to motivate cooperative people adequately today. The Good News therefore calls for the Gethsemane union of all cooperative people, even today, with the Christ who obediently suffered the Roman cross in ancient times. If we omit this union, the cross of Christ loses its divine redemptive power for people today, however attentive and even emotional their response to it is. The message of the cross then would be reduced to so much talk and emotional response, and the followers of Christ would lose their divine motivation from Gethsemane union with Christ.

Gethsemane union is not limited to an instant of time, because the full volitional redemption of humans requires ongoing, diachronic union with Christ. This fits with the plausible requirement that there be a starting point for the divine redemptive process in humans, and this requirement is crucially important, even if people have difficulty in identifying the starting point. Even so, humans habitually resist God and God's love-commands, and therefore an *ongoing* powerful and intentional, but noncoercive, antidote is needed. An event from history, even one's own personal history, will not supply the needed antidote, because no such event offers current *intentional guidance with the power of agapē*. An inward agent, however, can serve the purpose of divine redemption for humans, particularly the need of intentional guidance with the power in question.

The needed antidote comes from the inward Spirit of Christ who invites and encourages a receptive person to cry, with submission, "Abba! Father!" as Christ himself did in Gethsemane. The direction of this prayerful cry was, and is, to yield one's will to God's perfect will, and this cry is a repeatable episode, as needed by humans habitually alienated from God. The ongoing importance of Gethsemane, then, is not just as a moral context where humans obey a divine command. Instead, Gethsemane becomes a repeated context, even an ongoing life, where the risen Christ invites, encourages, and empowers one to yield into reconciliation and reverent companionship with God as one's ongoing "Abba, Father." Every occasion of human decision-making can become a Gethsemane context, courtesy of the inward Christ who values process (the *how*) as well as product (the *what*), but this is no suggestion of human perfection in this life (see Phil. 3:12).

Gethsemane union with Christ, although rigorously volitional, is grace-centered, because it revolves around God's unearned offer and sustenance of companionship with receptive humans. As indicated, one must "work out" this union for salvation in rigorous struggle against anti-God ways, but such "working out" is volitional cooperation with God that differs from "works" as a means of earning or meriting salvation from God (cf. Rom. 4:4). Accordingly, Paul describes himself as struggling according to all of the energy that God empowers in him (Col. 1:29).

No Pelagian threat will arise here, as long as we distinguish the terms for *offering* a gift (for instance, completely unearned) from the conditions for *appropriating* the gift (for instance, cooperation of receptive humans with God). A requirement of active human cooperation with God, after the model of Jesus in Gethsemane, does not entail a requirement of human earning, despite widespread confusions in this area (as Chapter 4 noted). An unearned gift, as suggested, can come with rigorous expectations for humans and severe conditions for human appropriation.

TOWARD CHRISTIAN PHILOSOPHY

If being Christian consists in Gethsemane union with Christ, then what follows for Christian *philosophy*? If Christian philosophy is genuinely *Christian*, it should follow suit in somehow representing or accommodating Gethsemane union with God in Christ. Paul remarks that "knowledge puffs up, but love builds up" (1 Cor. 8:1), and he could have added that *philosophy* (or any other human pursuit apart from God's authority, for that matter) puffs up, too. Accordingly, he reports that he does not trade in "eloquent wisdom, so that the cross of Christ might not be emptied of its power" (1 Cor. 1:17). This suggests that a philosophy can empty the power from the cross of Christ. Paul has in mind the *redemptive* power of the cross, as he immediately mentions the cross as "the power of

God" for "us who are being saved" (1 Cor. 1:18). How, then, can a philosophy empty the redemptive power of the cross of Christ? The answer is this: it can do so in *many* ways, given that there are many ways to mislead and obstruct people regarding God.

Paul has in mind, at least, the tendency of the world's wisdom and philosophy to obscure or divert attention from the reality of "Christ [as] the power of God and the wisdom of God" (1 Cor. 1:24). One such diversion occurs when a philosophy, perhaps even a philosophy called "Christian," ignores the redemptive importance of Gethsemane union with the inward Christ. If attention is directed away from such union, as with most philosophy, one easily can neglect the importance of such union for human redemption. In particular, one easily can ignore a human inquirer's being under question by God, relative to God's perfect will. This would be to ignore what Chapter 3 called "divine corrective inquiry" toward humans.

A test question arises for any proposed Christian philosophy: does the philosophy uphold the importance of one's obediently dying with Christ under the guiding agent-power of God as "Abba, Father"? If not, then the philosophy misses the mark as a distinctly Christian philosophy. Most philosophy fails this redemptive litmus test, because redemption, as being saved by God, is ignored by most philosophers, who thus fail to honor the unique redemptive Mediator from God, the inward Christ. We have, then, a sharp contrast between distinctly Christian philosophy and the many alternatives in circulation. Given God's unique moral character and will, we should not expect a broad philosophical unification with the alternatives (on which see Moser 2010a, chap. 5).

Aside from the diversionary dangers of philosophy, Paul acknowledges that "among the mature we do speak wisdom, though it is not a wisdom of this age" (1 Cor. 2:6). He would add that among the mature we do offer a philosophy, though it is not of this age. He has in mind the era of the risen Christ whose Good News is that people of all nations are called by God into the lasting life of union with God in Christ. A philosophy of the era of Christ is distinctively Christian, because it gives preeminence to the risen Christ with whom people are to share Gethsemane union. This preeminence includes giving pride of place to Christ and hence to redemption in Gethsemane union with him. The neglect of such preeminence entails neglect of a distinctly Christian philosophy. We have, then, a rather straightforward litmus test for a Christian philosophy, courtesy of the importance of Gethsemane union.

Christian philosophy joins Gethsemane union with a religious epistemology oriented toward the Spirit of God and Christ. As Chapter 3 suggested, Christian philosophy must find knowledge of God, like human redemption, in divine grace rather than in human earning. In particular, a Christian philosophy must acknowledge that the things of God are taught by God's Spirit, the Spirit of Christ, and not by "human wisdom." Paul thus states that "we have received the Spirit that is from God, so that we may understand the gifts bestowed on us by God" (1 Cor. 2:12).

In making Christ preeminent in all things, even in wisdom and philosophy, God does not allow the world to know God by its own wisdom. Paul remarks: "in the wisdom of God, the world did not know God through [its] wisdom" (1 Cor. 1:21). Instead, according to Paul, "Christ Jesus … became for us wisdom from God, and righteousness and sanctification and redemption" (1 Cor. 1:30; cf. Col. 2:3). The latter treasures are offered by divine grace but are appropriated by us only in the rigorous struggle of Gethsemane union with Christ. The latter struggle depends, of course, on our willingness to cooperate in the difficult, but life-giving redemptive process. So, our redemptive challenge is volitional, and not purely intellectual.

A Christian philosophy, as suggested, must accommodate the heart of what it is to be Christian, namely Gethsemane union with God in Christ as Lord. Otherwise, the philosophy does not merit the title "Christian." The union in question is no mere correct belief that something about Christ is true. Instead, it calls for volitional cooperation and companionship with Christ, who empowers and guides *how* we think, not just *what* we think. Accordingly, the rare fruit of the Spirit of Christ – love, joy, peace, patience, gentleness, and so on – should apply even to Christian thinking and thinkers. Divine redemption values the inward process of human cooperation and companionship with Christ as much as any objective reality. Christian philosophy should follow suit, under the preeminence of God in Christ. It also should acknowledge that communing with and obeying God can awaken one to otherwise neglected realities and evidence of God, as God emerges more clearly as "Abba, Father" in one's experience (see Mackintosh 1938a; cf. Mackintosh 1929, p. 55).

We face a serious problem: the frequent divorce of Christian belief and philosophy from the Christian foundation of the inward Christ and Gethsemane union with God in Christ. The result is correct intellectual belief without the needed divine power, guidance, and companionship from the inward Christ. In that case, even if one talks voluminously of Christ, one's moral agency does not underwrite that talk by witnessing to the powerful *agapē* character of Christ within oneself. People are left, then, with a conflicted witness at best, that is, with talk in the absence of the corresponding agent power of *agapē*. Christians thus begin to look and act a lot like the world, regardless of their extensive talk to the contrary. Talk, however, is cheap indeed.

Christian philosophy cannot be *merely* academic or impersonal, because it cannot abstract from questions and facts about our deepest motives and our personal standing before God in Christ. Some philosophers object to bringing Gethsemane union into Christian philosophy, on the ground that we should keep philosophy personally *impartial* and not make it confessional in any way. Specifically, the philosophy classroom, in this common view, is no place for personal confession or redemption. This view is puzzling, however, because it suggests that we should do Christian philosophy without attending to the key redemptive *reality* of being Christian in union with Christ, beyond the mere *notion* of being Christian. Impersonal talk, however, is too cheap and easy for Christian wisdom and philosophy. It leaves Christian philosophy as redemptively impotent as secular philosophy. Philosophy needs redeeming, and that by God in Christ, via divine–human Gethsemane union.

A Christian philosophy may prompt an inquirer to ask why he or she lacks evidence reported by some followers of Christ, such as the evidence of the inward flood of *agapē* from God's Spirit. This question will invite motivational issues about one's desires and intentions with regard to God in Christ, such as the question whether I am *willing* to yield reverently with Christ to God in Gethsemane. Have I hardened my heart to God in Christ? Alternatively, am I truly willing to submit to, and cooperate with, the authority of divine *agapē* in Christ, even if my academic peers take sharp exception and offer ridicule and rejection? If we avoid the latter question of divine authority in Christ, then we will not accommodate the distinctive religious epistemology in Christian philosophy (on which, see Chapter 3; cf. Moser 2008, 2010a). A philosophy can be more or less Christian, but if it omits the preeminence of Christ and the redemptive feature of Gethsemane union with Christ, it is Christian in name only. So, the fact that a person of a Christian persuasion formulates a philosophy, even about God, does not make the philosophy Christian.

Part of the distinctive content of a Christian philosophy arises from reflection on the preeminence of Christ and redemptive union with God in Christ, but a qualification is needed. Human reflection can stem from motives contrary to the divine love-commands exemplified in Christ. In that case, we will lack robust Christian philosophy, even if we have an intellectual skeleton of the true article. Christian philosophy must be continuous with the rigorous moral and spiritual content of the Good News of God in Christ.

If one pursues philosophy just to gain understanding, acquire truth, avoid error, or show off one's intellectual skills, rather than in the Gethsemane spirit from and for God in Christ, one is not doing robust Christian philosophy, anchored in Christlike motives and Gethsemane prayer. This suggests an indispensable moral and spiritual standard for Christian philosophy, courtesy of the Christ who is wisdom, righteousness, and redemption from God. In Christ himself we find the desired standard, because in him we find both *how* Christian philosophy is to be done (anchored in the Gethsemane prayer to "Abba, Father") and *what* (better, *whom*) such philosophy should regard as preeminent (Gethsemane union with God in Christ). This standard narrows Christian philosophy, as we should expect, and it fits with the acknowledged personal authority of such philosophy: Christ himself.

In Christian philosophy, God as the supreme and perfect authority ultimately testifies to himself, via the Spirit of the risen Christ, who is God's own image. Neither claims nor subjective experiences are self-attesting, but God as an intentional causal agent, with purposive power, is self-attesting in being self-manifesting and self-witnessing regarding God's and Christ's reality and character. This has major implications for Christian epistemology, and may be called, in the language of Chapter 3, *divine corrective inquiry* or (following James

S. Stewart 1940) *the divine self-verification of Christ in conscience*. As Chapter 3 indicated, Stewart sums up the latter verification as follows: "you begin exploring the fact of Christ, perhaps merely intellectually and theologically – and before you know where you are, the fact is exploring *you*, spiritually and morally ... That is the self-verification of Jesus." Philosophers can and should welcome this experienced reality, unashamedly and confidently. The need is long overdue, and the result is altogether illuminating for religious experience and foundational evidence of God (see Chapter 3 for details).

Through the Spirit of Christ, God manifests his own character of *agapē* in (the experience of) receptive humans, pouring out his power of enemy-love in their hearts. This is something only God can do; mere humans and counterfeit gods, including imaginary gods, lack the needed power and moral character and will. If something lacks this distinctive power, it will not be able to circulate it. Being *sui generis* on this front, God should be expected by us to be self-attesting, self-witnessing, and self-authenticating.

No agent other than God has the self-sufficient *agapē* character of enemy-love needed for the task in question. Accordingly, no agent other than God is either worthy of worship or divinely self-manifesting and self-authenticating. God's self-attesting yields a divine corrective inquiry in our receptive experience, particularly in our conscience, whereby we are challenged to move toward enemy-love and forgiveness in companionship with God, away from our destructive selfishness, pride, and despair (see Chapter 3). Ultimately, then, we humans do not convince people regarding God. *God* does, and we contribute by being in Gethsemane union with God in Christ, thereby manifesting the power (beyond the mere talk) of God's own perfect moral character. The rigor of Gethsemane union in our lives becomes, then, an important opportunity for manifesting and offering God's severe redemptive power to others.

The idea of God's offering, as a gracious and powerful gift, what the divine love-commands require of humans is central to the Good News of God's redemption as "the power of God for salvation to everyone who has faith [in God]" (Rom. 1:16). This idea fits with the emphasis of Jesus on God's gratuitous provision toward humans (Matt. 20:1–16, Luke 15:11–32). The provision acknowledges that the divine love-commands require a kind of power among humans that only a perfectly loving God can supply. The love commands of Jesus call for *companionship relationships* of unselfish love between oneself and God and between oneself and other humans. Such relationships go beyond mere actions to attitudes and to volitional fellowship, cooperation, and communion between and among personal agents, with God at the center as the ultimate source of power for *agapē*.

Going beyond right action, the divine love-commands challenge and form who we are and how we exist in the presence of God in Christ. They correctively judge humans by calling them up short by God's morally perfect standard, and then call humans to obedient redefinition, even "new creation," by the divine gift of companionship with God in Christ. Willing humans move beyond mere discussion, then, to rigorous personal transformation in an obedient relationship of reverent companionship with the God who intensely values the redemption of humans.

How, then, is Jesus Christ relevant to philosophy as a discipline? I will mention just one important way. Philosophy in its normal mode, without being receptive to authoritative divine love-commands, leaves humans in a discussion mode, short of an obedience mode under divine authority. Philosophical questions naturally prompt philosophical questions about philosophical questions, and this launches a regress of higher-order, or at least related, questions, with no end to philosophical discussion. Hence, the questions of philosophy seem, notoriously, perennial, as they resist closure for humans.

As divinely appointed Lord, Jesus commands humans to move, for their own good, to an obedience mode of existence relative to divine love-commands and God's perfect moral character and will. He thereby points humans to his perfectly loving Father who ultimately underwrites the divine love-commands for humans, for the sake of divine–human companionship. This is very different from yet another philosophical proposal. Accordingly, we need to transcend a normal discussion mode, and thus philosophical discussion itself, to face with sincerity the personal inward Authority who commands what humans need: faithful obedience and belonging to the perfectly loving Giver of life. Such obedience and belonging of the heart (in kardiatheology) provide the way humans are to *receive* the gift of divine *agapē*. Insofar as the discipline of philosophy becomes guided, in terms of its pursuits, by that gift on offer, it becomes kerygma-oriented in virtue of becoming an enabler of the Good News of God in Christ. This is very different from philosophy as commonly practiced, even among Christian theorists.

Many philosophers ignore or oppose Jesus, because he transcends a familiar, honorific discussion mode, and demands that they do the same. Philosophical discussion becomes advisable and permissible, under the divine love-commands, if and only if it honors those commands by compliance with them. Given God's self-sacrificial love toward us, Jesus commands love from us toward God and others *beyond* discussion and the acquisition of truth, even philosophical truth. He thereby cleanses the temple of philosophy and turns over our self-promoting tables of mere philosophical discussion. He pronounces judgment on this long-standing self-made temple, in genuine love for its wayward builders. His corrective judgment purportedly brings us what we truly need to flourish in lasting companionship with God and other humans. We now can see that Jesus bears significantly on philosophy as a discipline (and on related truth- and wisdom-seeking disciplines as well).

The remaining question for us is volitional, from Gethsemane: are we *willing* to participate in the powerful life of God in Christ, in God's unselfish love even toward enemies? I offer no bet on the final answer now, but I do want to set aside a long-standing objection from supposed human evidence that bars belief in God.

EVIDENCE BEYOND ATHEISM

Evidential atheism, as espoused by various philosophical atheists, recommends belief that God does not exist on the basis of not just the evidence of which we are aware, but also our overall *available* evidence. Such atheism would count against the evidential position of this chapter (and Chapter 3, too). This section identifies a widely neglected problem from potential surprise evidence that under-mines an attempt to give a cogent justification of such evidential atheism. In addition, it contends that evidential agnosticism fares better than evidential atheism relative to this neglected problem and that traditional monotheism has evidential resources, unavailable to evidential atheism, that promise to save it from the fate of evidential atheism. We thus shall raise a serious evidential problem for cogently justifying atheism and identify why traditional monotheism need not succumb to the same problem.

Some options

Atheism comes in many flavors. The most common is *simple* atheism:

SA. God does not exist.

A more complex flavor is *evidential* atheism:

EA. Owing to the direction of our overall available evidence, we should believe that God does not exist.

Doxastic atheism, in contrast, states the following:

DA. Some people believe that God does not exist.

Someone accepting either SA or DA can consistently (if oddly) say: I believe that God does not exist, but I have no view regarding the status of our overall available evidence regarding God's existence and thus no view regarding EA. A person could endorse simple or doxastic atheism, then, without being an evidential atheist. Evidential atheists, however, are logically required to recommend belief that simple atheism is true, even if some of them fail actually to believe that God does not exist. The history of philosophy abundantly represents advocates of SA, EA, and DA. (For a recent case for evidential atheism, involving a claim to "show" that no epistemic reasons for belief in God are "available," see Martin 1990, p. 38; cf. pp. 11, 30, 33; for some additional proponents of atheism, see the thinkers mentioned in the historical discussions of Buckley 1987 and Hyman 2007.)

Simple theism entails the falsity of simple atheism; it states:

ST. God exists.

In addition, evidential theism states:

ET. Owing to the direction of our overall available evidence, we should believe that God exists.

ET entails that we should believe the opposite of what evidential atheism states that we should believe. Doxastic theism, in contrast, states:

DT. Some people believe that God exists.

Someone accepting either ST or DT can consistently say: I believe that God exists, but I have no view regarding the status of our overall available evidence regarding God's existence and thus no view regarding ET. Accordingly, a person could endorse simple or doxastic theism without being an evidential theist; some fideists appear to fit into this category (on fideism, see Moser 2010a, chap. 2). Evidential theists, however, must recommend that one believe that simple theism is true, even if some of them fail to believe that God exists.

If reality is just material bodies (large or small) in motion, then simple atheism is true, because God would not be just material bodies (large or small) in motion. This suggests a possible quick case for simple atheism, but a problem arises for this case, regardless of the actual truth-value of SA: we apparently lack decisive evidence for holding that reality is just material bodies in motion. At least, this is a topic of ongoing controversy among philosophers and others.

Another possible quick argument for simple atheism runs as follows: if God exists, the severe evil in the actual world would not exist; the actual world's severe evil does exist; so, God does not exist. Here, again, the case would not be decisive, because we have no decisive reason to think that God would not allow the severe evil in the actual world. Arguably, as the free-will defense (from Plantinga 1977 and others) implies, God could create various kinds of beings with free wills, and they could be causally responsible, directly or indirectly, for the severe evil in the actual world.

A noteworthy problem arises from our limited evidential resources concerning divine purposes. We humans are simply not in a position to know that God would not allow the severe evil in the actual world. Of course, God would be a moral tyrant, unworthy of worship, if God *caused* the severe evil in the actual world, but simple theism does not imply otherwise. We now can bracket, however, any evidential problem of evil for the sake of a different, less appreciated evidential problem.

Potential surprise evidence

A serious problem concerns whether evidential atheism allows for due evidential modesty for humans in the face of potential surprise evidence of God's existence. The problem is particularly vivid in a possible universe where (unbeknown to some) God actually intervenes, if unpredictably and elusively, in human experience. We might imagine that God intervenes elusively with divine corrective inquiry (as characterized in Chapter 3) to some people in this universe. (This problem, however, does not assume that God exists in the actual universe.) Accordingly, some people will ask, regarding EA, whether we ever reasonably can suppose that we have canvassed *all available evidence* in a way that calls for our believing that God does not exist. Such canvassing seems to be a tall order, particularly in connection with the issue of God's nonexistence, given our real limits in canvassing all available evidence regarding God's existence. As a result, it might seem doubtful that we can reasonably recommend our believing that God does not exist.

Part of the problem lies in the vagueness of our talk of "available evidence." Although available evidence can vary among persons, we should not assume that our ordinary talk of "available evidence" offers a precise specification for the "availability" of evidence. Taking "available" in a rather liberal sense, we can ask whether it is always the case that one's turning the next corner, so to speak, could yield "available" surprising, salient evidence of God's existence that is undefeated. If currently undisclosed evidence just around the next corner is part of our overall available evidence, then the actual direction of our overall available evidence of God's existence will be potentially elusive with regard to atheism. In other words, the disclosure of previously undisclosed available evidence in favor of God's existence could defeat prior support for atheism that discounted this evidence, and we apparently have no basis to rule out such disclosure in our available evidence. (On the function of evidential defeaters in general, see Moser 1989; cf. Pollock and Cruz 1999.)

We should distinguish "canvassing all of our available evidence" from "the direction of our overall available evidence." Evidential atheism does not require our "canvassing all of our available evidence" or our canvassing any evidence, for that matter. Instead, on the basis of the direction of our overall available evidence, it recommends that we should believe that God does not exist. Our overall available evidence can point in a specific direction without our canvassing this evidence to identify the specific direction indicated. For instance, my available evidence can indicate the presence of a gnat in my grapefruit juice although I fail to identify this indication, perhaps as a result of a distraction. More generally, what our evidence indicates does not depend on what *we identify* our evidence to indicate. A contrary view would risk a level confusion between what our evidence indicates and what we identify our evidence to indicate.

The plot thickens if we seek to justify (that is, to *give* a justification for) evidential atheism and thus to go beyond a claim to EA's being true or to one's *having* evidence that justifies EA. In that case, we have to ask about *confirming* the direction of our overall available evidence regarding God's nonexistence. An answer will be elusive if we face elusiveness in what our overall available evidence actually includes regarding God's nonexistence. More specifically, given that we could confront available salient evidence for God's existence around the next corner, an attempt to justify EA apparently faces a problem. We cannot cogently, or persuasively, tell if our total available evidence lacks undefeated evidence of God's existence as long as our available evidence includes *currently undisclosed* available evidence. So far as we can cogently tell, the latter available evidence could include salient undefeated evidence of God's existence. (Here we can allow for the possibility of various ways in which God provides salient evidence of God's existence in human experience, including through the kind of divine corrective inquiry identified in Chapter 3.)

If we were to exclude currently undisclosed evidence from our available evidence, we would implausibly collapse the notion of available evidence into the notion of *actually possessed* evidence. This would be unacceptable, particularly if we aimed to consider an evidential assessment that bears on our overall available evidence, including evidence we do not yet possess but readily could or will come to possess. We often seek to assess not just the disclosed evidence one actually possesses but also the broader evidence available to one, that is, the evidence one could come to possess without undue difficulty. A case for evidential atheism that concerns only disclosed evidence one possesses, and cannot withstand broader available evidence, would lack a kind of epistemic resilience that we value and often seek. Accordingly, evidential atheism would sacrifice epistemic resilience in retreating from available evidence to a more limited base of only disclosed evidence one possesses.

The problem at hand concerns not the truth of atheism or even one's *having* evidence that justifies atheism, but rather one's *cogently justifying* atheism. In reply, one might propose the following: whatever the conditions that justify simple atheism, if those conditions are satisfied by one's case, or argument, for the justification of simple atheism, then one has justified simple atheism. Suppose that some feature, F, is sufficient for the justification of simple atheism (in the absence of defeaters). Perhaps F is either some kind of doxastic coherence, some kind of experiential feature, or some combination of the previous two features. In addition, if one's *case* for the justification of simple atheism (beyond its being true) possesses F, then one may infer that one's case is justified, on the ground that F is sufficient for justification (in the absence of defeaters). This position properly allows for a distinction between the justification of (= the evidence that justifies) simple atheism and the justification of *a case*, or *an argument*, for simple atheism, given that simple atheism is not itself an argument at all.

We should grant that F's adequacy in the justification of (= the evidence that justifies) simple atheism can be paralleled by F's adequacy in the justification of *a case* for simple atheism. Accordingly, F could be a feature that confers justification not only on a simple proposition, such as SA, but also on an argument for that simple proposition. Even so, the justification of a case need not be a *cogent* justification, because it need not be a justification that avoids begging a key question under dispute.

A key disputed question facing EA is whether our currently *undisclosed* available evidence includes salient undefeated evidence of God's existence. Proponents of EA will beg a key question if they simply assume a negative answer to that question. In addition, they will do the same if they offer a simple inductive inference based on their currently disclosed evidence compatible with atheism. The latter inference will beg the key disputed question of whether our currently undisclosed available evidence regarding God's existence agrees with the direction of an evidential atheist's currently disclosed evidence with regard to God's existence.

We plausibly can distinguish between what is justified *relative to F* regarding atheism and what is justified *relative to our total available evidence* regarding atheism. The latter evidence would encompass any available defeaters of evidence for atheism (including defeaters in currently undisclosed available evidence) that would be neglected by the more restricted evidence consisting of F. Accordingly, we can ask whether one can cogently justify the nonexistence claim of atheism – that is, the claim that God does not exist – relative to our undisclosed available evidence *and* our disclosed evidence.

The problem is not in cogently justifying a nonexistence claim in general. Instead, the problem is in cogently justifying a nonexistence claim relative to undisclosed available evidence in a particular kind of context: namely, a context where many (otherwise) reasonable and trustworthy people report their having experiential evidence for the opposing claim that God exists. The latter context, so far as we can tell, offers the evidentially live potential that undisclosed available evidence includes an undefeated defeater for any disclosed evidence for atheism. In addition, the context includes (otherwise) reasonable people who plausibly will raise the question of whether an atheist's undisclosed available evidence includes an undefeated defeater for disclosed evidence for atheism. As a result, the serious matter of begging a key question naturally arises. The problem at hand, then, is not a general problem regarding the cogent justifying of a claim that something does not exist. The current problem for cogently justifying atheism offers nothing against cogently justifying a claim that unicorns, for instance, do not exist.

We can clarify the problem by comparing a case for evidential atheism and a case for evidential agnosticism. Such agnosticism states:

> EG. Owing to the (highly mixed) direction of our overall evidence, we should withhold judgment (neither affirm nor deny) that God exists.

A common motivation for agnostics is to avoid error or at least to minimize the risk of error. If relevant evidence about God's existence is highly mixed, then in answering either yes or no to the question of whether God exists, one seriously risks falling into error. The better alternative, according to agnostics, is to refrain from answering either yes or no (that is, to withhold judgment), because this can save one from error. (For a popular variation on evidential agnosticism, see Russell 1953.)

Clearly, one pays a price in adopting EG: one then will miss out on an opportunity to acquire a truth. Either it is true that God exists or it is true that God does not exist. Agnostics forgo acquiring a truth in this area of reality, while holding that evidential atheists go too far in the negative direction and evidential theists go too far in the positive direction (at least relative to agnostics' evidence). In contrast, evidential atheism entails that evidential theism and evidential agnosticism make the wrong recommendation on the basis of our evidence. It implies that our overall available evidence counts decisively against simple theism.

Suppose, as appears to be so, that we cannot cogently tell if our total available evidence lacks undefeated evidence of God's existence, given that our available evidence includes currently undisclosed available evidence. As far as we can cogently tell, our undisclosed available evidence actually could include salient undefeated evidence of God's existence (such as the kind found in divine corrective inquiry). Although this lesson raises a problem for a cogent case for EA, a case for EG can accommodate it, because EG recommends simply withholding judgment that God exists on the basis of our overall evidence.

More specifically, a case for EG can avoid begging a key question begged by a case for EA: the question of whether our undisclosed available evidence includes salient undefeated evidence of God's existence. A case for EG can leave this question wide open, while affirming that we lack the evidential resources to give either a cogent negative answer or a cogent positive answer. In this respect, EG is evidentially preferable to EA.

Regarding undisclosed available evidence, evidential agnostics can offer the following advice: withhold judgment until the relevant evidence is actually disclosed. This is in keeping with the statement of EG regarding simply our overall evidence rather than our overall available evidence. Accordingly, one could argue that, from an evidential point of view, advocates of EA should forsake their atheism for the more resilient and evidentially safe position of evidential agnosticism. EA, then, is not epistemically stable relative to its being cogently justified in competition with EG.

One might counter now that advocates of EA should retreat from the broader base of our overall *available* evidence to the narrower base of our overall disclosed evidence, in keeping with EG. I have suggested, however, that this would remove a certain kind of epistemic resilience that we value and often seek: namely, the ability of a position to withstand our broader available evidence, beyond the disclosed evidence we possess. In any case, atheists, such as Martin 1990, often invoke our overall "available" evidence in a manner that does not limit their position to our actually disclosed evidence relative to our overall available evidence. In favoring such a rigid limit, atheists would leave us with a position that has a relatively timid evidential scope, particularly regarding undisclosed available evidence. We might call such a position *restricted* evidential atheism, to distinguish it from the bolder version represented by EA. Such restricted atheism amounts to agnosticism, rather than atheism, regarding our undisclosed available evidence. In this respect, it involves a retreat from the evidential atheism of EA (and, for instance, of Martin 1990).

Evidence and attitudes

Let's highlight the problem of cogently justifying EA in connection with two variations, *neutral* evidential atheism and *positive* evidential atheism:

NEA. Owing to the direction of our overall available evidence, we should believe that God does not exist, while we remain neutral on whether it is good that God does not exist.

PEA. Owing to the direction of our overall available evidence, we should believe that God does not exist, while we deem it good that God does not exist.

An advocate of PEA could share the following views of Thomas Nagel noted in Chapter 2: "I want atheism to be true … I hope there is no God. I don't want there to be a God; I don't want the universe to be like that" (1997, p. 130). We also could distinguish a version of evidential atheism that includes our deeming it bad that God does not exist, but NEA and PEA will serve our purpose now.

Unlike PEA, NEA does not include a judgment in favor of the goodness of God's nonexistence. Likewise, NEA does not include a judgment in favor of the badness of God's nonexistence. In this regard, it recommends neutrality. We apparently have no way to show that such neutrality is impossible for humans. On the contrary, it seems to be a live option, even if many people actually lack such neutrality.

Advocates of PEA face a serious but widely neglected problem in any attempt to give a cogent justification of their evidential agnosticism. The problem stems from the live prospect of intentional divine elusiveness if a God worthy of worship exists (on which see Moser 2008). Such elusiveness would include at least the following: God typically would hide God's existence from people ill disposed toward it, in order not to antagonize these people in a way that diminishes their ultimate receptivity toward God's character and purposes. As a result, we should expect evidence of God's existence typically to be hidden from advocates of PEA; so, *their* lacking such evidence is not by itself the basis of a case for atheism. Advocates of PEA should expect their disclosed evidence of God's existence to be potentially misleading as a result of God's being purposive and selective (if God exists) in disclosing salient available evidence of God's existence. God's relevant purpose would be to enhance the prospects of redemption for certain humans at an opportune time, such as when they are more receptive toward God.

In virtue of being worthy of worship and thus morally perfect, as Chapter 1 indicated, the God in question would seek from humans more than their intellectual assent to the proposition that God exists. God would also seek a receptive, cooperative human attitude toward a divine moral character worthy of worship. In other words, as suggested, God would seek trust in God, and not mere faith that God exists. When people are not yet ready to adopt such an attitude, God reasonably could hide divine evidence from them so as not to repel them further away from God in their responses to God. Such divine hiding is acknowledged by the major monotheistic traditions, and it figures in some contemporary work on theistic epistemology (see, for instance, Chapter 3; Moser 2008, 2010a).

The previous consideration raises a problem for any attempt to give a cogent justification of evidential atheism in conjunction with PEA. The problem concerns not a lack of overall available evidence but rather a human attitude toward God's existence that potentially interferes with God's purposive disclosing of evidence for divine existence. This problem extends the general problem for EA identified previously to any variation on EA that includes PEA.

One could argue that the same extended problem applies to NEA, but I shall not digress to this matter. The needed argument would rest on the view that God would have an attitude of withdrawal toward human neutrality about the goodness of God's existence; this would be similar to God's attitude toward the human response of PEA. This view would gain plausibility from a case for the following position: for redemptive purposes, God would seek a human attitude of cooperative receptivity toward God's existence and character and thus would typically hide from people who are not ready to adopt such an agreeable attitude. This approach to NEA is not implausible, but it is independent of the present argument.

Consequences for theism

We have seen that, for better or worse, the role of potential surprise available evidence pushes evidential atheists toward evidential agnosticism as an epistemically better option. We should ask if theists share the same fate from potential surprise evidence.

Let's distinguish *logical* from *evidential* exclusion of defeaters. It seems clear that, given any disclosed evidence for God's existence, we cannot *logically* exclude potential surprise defeaters of this evidence in one's overall available evidence. At least, I can find no way to do so, and I find no hope in any ontological argument (on which, see Moser 2010a, chap. 3; cf. Oppy 1995). For instance, the disclosing of one's hitherto-undisclosed available evidence logically could bring *nothing but* an unending, uninterrupted onslaught of pointless and excruciating suffering for all concerned. We plausibly may think of the realization of such a logically possible dark prospect as yielding an undefeated defeater for any previously disclosed evidence for God's existence. I, for one, think of it as doing so, because it strongly calls into question the reality of a God who cares for people in virtue of divine moral perfection. Accordingly, I regard the claim that God exists to be logically contingent and (in principle) falsifiable, but not actually falsified or false.

The mere logical prospect of the defeater in question does not yield an actual defeater of any experiential evidence for theism. (A mere logical possibility does not a defeater make, at least when the contingent evidence regarding a contingent claim is at stake.)

The prospect of the defeater would need to be *realized* in one's experience for an actual defeater (of the sort imagined) to arise. As a result, this prospect does not push theists toward evidential agnosticism. Theists still can have their experiential evidence for theism, and this evidence still can be unaccompanied by actual undefeated defeaters. It follows, so far as this case goes, that one logically can have evidence that justifies theism.

What of the cogent justifying of evidential theism (ET)? Does this meet the same troubled fate as EA? The answer depends on whether undisclosed evidence available to theists could be an obstacle to a cogent justification of ET. Here we move from logical to evidential exclusion of defeaters. The key question becomes: can theists cogently tell if their total available evidence lacks an undefeated defeater of their evidence for God's existence?

The answer will depend on what kind of evidence of God's existence theists actually have. If one's evidence for theism amounts to evidence for a kind of deism that does not offer (evidence of) testimonial evidence from God concerning one's future, then the fate of EA appears to be a genuine threat for ET as well. In that case, one apparently will lack the evidence needed for evidential exclusion of the defeater in question. That is, this defeater will be an evidentially live option relative to one's evidence for deism.

The claims of traditional monotheism differ significantly from deism. Such monotheism, whether in Judaism, Christianity, or Islam, offers purported evidence of God's promise not to abandon God's people to ultimate futility. One can argue that this future-involving evidence offers an *evidential* (but not a logical) exclusion of the defeater arising from the aforementioned dark prospect. At least, many monotheists would argue thus, and their case may recruit abductive considerations relative to their experience (on which, see Moser 2008, pp. 63–69; cf. Wiebe 2004, chap. 3). Aside from the details of their arguments, they do have purported evidential resources to undermine the *evidential* threat of such a defeater, despite the *logical* possibility of the dark prospect in question. In this respect, traditional monotheism can make use of purported evidential resources unavailable to atheism. (Clearly, however, this section cannot entertain all of the alleged defeaters facing evidence for traditional monotheism; nor therefore can it develop a full cogent case for such monotheism.)

Of course, atheists cannot consistently make an appeal to future-involving evidence purportedly from a divine knower, but traditional monotheists can, and often do. As a result, the kind of potential surprise evidence that undermines a cogent justification of evidential atheism will not automatically undermine a cogent justification of traditional monotheism. If monotheists can vouchsafe a favorable promise from God, they have an opportunity to undermine the dark defeater in question. (The exact development of this opportunity would take us far beyond the scope of this section, but it could make effective use of the kind of divine corrective inquiry and reciprocity noted in Chapter 3.) It follows further that the demand for a cogent justification relative to our overall available evidence need not push evidential monotheism toward agnosticism in the challenging way it pushes evidential atheism.

Evidential atheists in search of a cogent justification for their atheism must face the difficult lesson identified here: their position lacks the evidential resources to be cogently justified and is evidentially inferior to evidential agnosticism. We may describe the problem as the *undermining* of the case for evidential atheism. A retreat to simple atheism will not make the problem go away, because questions about a cogent case for simple atheism are inevitable and worthy of serious attention. Atheists, then, are well advised to reconsider agnosticism or monotheism, for the sake of improved evidential stability.

A challenge to agnostics must be more complex and subtle, given that they do not stick their necks out as far as evidential atheists do. It will question whether agnostics are genuinely receptive to the kind of evidence appropriate to a God worthy of worship. In particular, it will ask whether they are sincerely open to (receive and cooperate with) divine corrective inquiry. If they are not, God may choose to hide from them for redemptive purposes. If they are sincerely open, we can ask about what this openness involves in their lives. One issue is whether they are genuinely seeking for God on God's vigorous redemptive terms, relative to the kind of evidence fitting for God. If they are, God will be able to supply the needed evidence at the opportune time, with the kind of divine self-authentication noted in Chapter 3. The case of agnostics is, at any rate, significantly different from the case for evidential atheism.

CONCLUSION

According to this chapter, and this book, Christian philosophy and life depend on Christian spirituality, because they require our discerning God in Christ for our ultimate authority and redemption, in philosophy as in life with God. This discerning is not casual or speculative at all, but in receptivity to divine corrective inquiry it requires volitional cooperation with God, which in turn depends on Christ's Gethsemane prayer: "Abba, Father … not what I want, but what You want" (Mark 14:36). If we fail to make this prayer our own, in an ongoing manner, we fail to enter into robust Christian philosophy and even Christian life with God. The indispensable role of such Gethsemane prayer underwrites the central role for Christian spirituality in Christian philosophy and life. It also prompts us to reconceive religion and philosophy in at least the areas covered in this book, including the methodology and epistemology regarding God, the significance of flux in human life, the divine salvation of humans, and the nature of philosophy under the severely redemptive God.

The "Gethsemane priority" mentioned in Chapter 4, whereby one makes God's perfect, redemptive will a priority in one's life, stems only from the kind of Gethsemane prayer in question. James S. Stewart has put the key lesson as follows:

Often [people] tell you that they do not pray because Christ is not real to them. The truth of the matter is, Christ is not real to them because they do not pray. To the [person] who never prays, God in Christ cannot make Himself real [to that person]. To the soul which will never subdue its noisy clamour to silence, to listen for the divine voice which guides and blesses and reassures, there is little hope that a convincing religious experience will ever come. But … to the [person] who keeps praying, Christ is sure to make Himself real, sure to become the biggest fact in life filling the whole horizon. (1937, pp. 61–62)

Stewart has in mind not human chatter toward God but Gethsemane prayer that is sincere about yielding to God as God. This is indeed a key difference between prayer and chatter.

If the Gethsemane-oriented approach of this book is on the right track, then Gethsemane prayer must be kept front and center in human relations to God, including in human knowing of God. This may not fit with much of traditional religion and philosophy, but no serious problem or objection thereby emerges. Instead, we have a case for reconceiving religion and philosophy. This is the main burden of this book, and it embraces the redemptive severity of God as something we should expect of a God worthy of worship. In this approach, religion and philosophy no longer can be business as usual, given the current and ongoing crisis of Gethsemane for all inquirers of God. The stakes are now raised high, rigorously high, for the sake of the divine redemption of humans. The next move, by way of a response to God in Gethsemane, is for human inquirers, whom God's *agapē* interventions invite to Gethsemane.

This book has emphasized severity and struggle for God and humans in the Gethsemane-oriented redemptive process and in the corresponding evidential process. It has done so as a needed corrective to cheap theism and cheap grace. The full story of the divine redemption of humans, however, has an additional component: the divine uplift of humans into the peace and the joy of new life with God in Christ. Accordingly, Paul characterizes the kingdom of God as consisting in not just righteousness but also "peace and joy in the Holy Spirit" (Rom. 14:17).

The vital divine uplift of humans via God's peace and joy occurs not as a replacement for the rigor of Gethsemane but instead as an accompanying reality in the midst of life's severity. Indeed, the connection between severity and uplift goes beyond what people ordinarily expect or even imagine. Strikingly, Paul claims: "We rejoice in our sufferings" (Rom. 5:3, RSV), and he offers as the ground of this strange rejoicing God's redemptive work in our sufferings, particularly God's forming people in the inward character of Christ, with endurance, character, and hope.

Paul finds no ultimate disappointment in the rigorous and hopeful process of redemption, because God already has done something striking in the experience of cooperative humans: God has flooded their motivational centers with divine *agapē*, and thereby made them new, in life with God in Christ. This book has put this humanly experienced reality front and center, for the sake of illuminating a key goal of the severity of God. This goal invites people to ask how, if at all, they value such *agapē*, and whether it is truly a Gethsemane priority for them. The answer will indicate whether *God* is actually a priority for them, that is, whether God is truly God for them. The stakes, then, are high indeed, given the reconceived, Gethsemane standards for religion and philosophy.

Bibliography

Baillie, John. 1956. *The Idea of Revelation in Recent Thought*. New York: Columbia University Press.

1963. *A Reasoned Faith*. London: Oxford University Press.

Barr, James. 1993. *Biblical Faith and Natural Theology*. Oxford: Clarendon Press.

Barth, Karl. 1933. *The Epistle to the Romans*, trans. E.C. Hoskyns. London: Oxford University Press.

Berkhof, Hendrikus. 1968. "Science and the Biblical World-View." In Ian Barbour, ed., *Science and Religion*, pp. 43–53. New York: Harper.

Best, Ernest. 1967. *The Letter of Paul to the Romans*. Cambridge University Press.

Bonhoeffer, Dietrich. 1937. *Discipleship: Dietrich Bonhoeffer Works*, vol. IV, trans. Barbara Green and Reinhard Krauss. Minneapolis, MN: Fortress Press, 2001.

Brunner, Emil. 1937. *The Divine Imperative*, trans. Olive Wyon. London: Lutterworth Press.

1950. *The Christian Doctrine of God*, trans. Olive Wyon. London: Lutterworth Press.

1957. *Faith, Hope, and Love*. Philadelphia, PA: Westminster Press.

1962. *The Christian Doctrine of the Church, Faith, and the Consummation*, trans. David Cairns. Philadelphia, PA: Westminster Press.

Buckley, Michael J. 1987. *At the Origins of Modern Atheism*. New Haven, CT: Yale University Press.

Bultmann, Rudolf. 1951. *Theology of the New Testament*, vol. I, trans. Kendrick Grobel. New York: Charles Scribner's Sons.

Byrnes, Michael. 2003. *Conformation to the Death of Christ and the Hope of Resurrection*. Rome: Gregorian University Press.

Campbell, Douglas A. 2009. *The Deliverance of God*. Grand Rapids, MI: Eerdmans.

Chesterton, G. K. 1927. "The Convert." In *The Collected Poems of G. K. Chesterton*. London: Palmer.

Clark, Kenneth W. 1935. "The Meaning of *Energeō* and *Katargeō* in the New Testament." *Journal of Biblical Literature*, 54, 93–101.

Cranfield, C. E. B. 1975. *The Epistle to the Romans*, 2 vols. Edinburgh: T&T Clark.

1991. "'The Works of the Law' in the Epistle to the Romans." *Journal for the Study of the New Testament*, 43, 89–101.

Daly, Robert J. 2009. *Sacrifice Unveiled: The True Meaning of Christian Sacrifice*. London: T&T Clark.

Das, A. Andrew. 2009. "Paul and Works of Obedience in Second Temple Judaism." *Catholic Biblical Quarterly*, 71, 795–812.

Duncan, George. 1934. *The Epistle of Paul to the Galatians*. New York: Harper.

Dunn, James D. G. 1985. "Works of the Law and the Curse of the Law." *New Testament Studies*, 31, 523–542.

1988. *Romans*, 2 vols. Dallas, TX: Word.

1998. *The Theology of Paul the Apostle*. Grand Rapids, MI: Eerdmans.

Farmer, Herbert H. 1939. *The Healing Cross*. New York: Charles Scribner's Sons.

Fiddes, Paul. 1988. *The Creative Suffering of God*. Oxford University Press.

Fitzmyer, Joseph A. 1992. *Romans: The Anchor Bible*. New York: Doubleday.

Furnish, Victor P. 1972. *The Love Command in the New Testament*. Nashville, TN: Abingdon Press.

Gorman, Michael J. 2001. *Cruciformity*. Grand Rapids, MI: Eerdmans.

2009. *Inhabiting the Cruciform God*. Grand Rapids, MI: Eerdmans.

Hanson, N. R. 1971. *What I Do Not Believe and Other Essays*. Dordrecht: Reidel.

Hays, Richard B. 1997. *First Corinthians*. Louisville, KY: John Knox.

Heschel, Abraham. 1962. *The Prophets*. New York: Jewish Publication Society.

1973. *A Passion for Truth*. New York: Farrar.

Hintikka, Jaakko. 1967. "Time, Truth, and Knowledge in Ancient Greek Philosophy." *American Philosophical Quarterly*, 4, 1–14.

Hoskyns, Edwyn C., and Francis Noel Davey. 1981. *Crucifixion-Resurrection: The Pattern of the Theology and Ethics of the New Testament*, ed. by Gordon S. Wakefield. London: SPCK.

Hubbard, Moyer V. 2002. *New Creation in Paul's Letters and Thought*. Cambridge University Press.

Hyman, Gavin. 2007. "Atheism in Modern History." In Michael Martin, ed., *The Cambridge Companion to Atheism*, pp. 27–46. Cambridge University Press.

Juergensmeyer, Mark. 2003. *Terror in the Mind of God*, 3rd edn. Berkeley, CA: University of California Press.

Kane, Robert, ed. 2005. *The Oxford Handbook of Free Will*. New York: Oxford University Press.

Käsemann, Ernst. 1971. *Perspectives on Paul*, trans. Margaret Kohl. Philadelphia, PA: Fortress Press.

   1980. *Commentary on Romans*, trans. G. W. Bromiley. Grand Rapids, MI: Eerdmans.

   2010. *On Being a Disciple of the Crucified Naʒarene*, trans. R. A. Harrisville, ed. by Rudolf Landau. Grand Rapids, MI: Eerdmans.

Kierkegaard, Søren. 1846. *Concluding Unscientific Postscript to Philosophical Fragments: Kierkegaard's Writings*, vol. XII, trans. H. V. Hong and E. H. Hong. Princeton University Press, 1992.

   1850. *Practice in Christianity: Kierkegaard's Writings*, vol. XX, trans. H. V. Hong and E. H. Hong. Princeton University Press, 1991.

   1851a. *For Self-Examination/Judge for Yourself! Kierkegaard's Writings*, vol. XXI, trans. H. V. Hong and E. H. Hong. Princeton University Press, 1990.

   1851b. *Søren Kierkegaard's Journals and Papers*, vol. I, trans. H. V. Hong and E. H. Hong. Bloomington, IN: Indiana University Press, 1967 (trans. of *JP*, vol. I, par. 993 slightly modified in quotation).

Kim, Seyoon. 2002. *Paul and the New Perspective*. Grand Rapids, MI: Eerdmans.

Klassen, William. 1984. *Love of Enemies*. Philadelphia, PA: Fortress Press.

Knight, George A. F. 1959. *A Christian Theology of the Old Testament*. London: SCM Press.

Mackintosh, H. R. 1912. *The Doctrine of the Person of Jesus Christ*. Edinburgh: T&T Clark.

1923. "*Unio Mystica* as a Theological Conception." In *Some Aspects of Christian Belief*, pp. 99–120. London: Hodder & Stoughton.

1927. *The Christian Experience of Forgiveness*. London: Nisbet Press.

1928. "Grace." In James Hastings, ed., *Encyclopedia of Religion and Ethics*, vol. V, pp. 364–367. New York: Charles Scribner's Sons.

1929. *The Christian Apprehension of God*. London: SCM Press.

1931. "The Motive and the Sum of Obedience." In *The Highway of God*, pp. 1–12. Edinburgh: T&T Clark.

1938a. "Obedience the Organ of Knowledge." In *Sermons*, pp. 113–122. Edinburgh: T&T Clark.

1938b. "An Indisputable Argument." In *Sermons*, pp. 171–179. Edinburgh: T&T Clark.

Martin, Michael. 1990. *Atheism: A Philosophical Justification*. Philadelphia, PA: Temple University Press.

Meadors, Edward. 2006. *Idolatry and the Hardening of the Heart*. London: T&T Clark.

Morris, Leon. 1981. *Testaments of Love*. Grand Rapids, MI: Eerdmans.

Moser, Paul K. 1989. *Knowledge and Evidence*. Cambridge University Press.

2008. *The Elusive God: Reorienting Religious Epistemology*. Cambridge University Press.

2010a. *The Evidence for God: Religious Knowledge Reexamined*. Cambridge University Press.

2010b. "*Agapēic* Theism." *European Journal for Philosophy of Religion*, 2, 1–18.

Moser, Paul K., and Mark McCreary. 2010. "Kierkegaard's Conception of God." *Philosophy Compass*, 5, 127–135.

Nagel, Thomas. 1971. "The Absurd." *Journal of Philosophy*, 63, 716–727. Reprinted in E. D. Klemke, ed., *The Meaning of Life*, pp. 151–161. New York: Oxford University Press, 1981. Reference is to this reprint.

1997. *The Last Word*. New York: Oxford University Press.

Nygren, Anders. 1953. *Agapē and Eros*, trans. P. S. Watson. New York: Harper & Row.

Oman, John. 1919. *Grace and Personality*, 2nd edn. Cambridge University Press.

1928. *Vision and Authority*, 2nd edn. London: Hodder & Stoughton.

Oppy, Graham. 1995. *Ontological Arguments and Belief in God*. Cambridge University Press.

Pascal, Blaise. 1669. *Pensées*, trans. A. J. Krailsheimer. London: Penguin, 1995.

Plantinga, Alvin. 1977. *God, Freedom, and Evil*. New York: Harper & Row.

Pollock, John, and Joseph Cruz. 1999. *Contemporary Theories of Knowledge*, 2nd edn. Lanham, MD: Rowman & Littlefield.

Quine, W. V. 1957. "The Scope and Language of Science." In *The Ways of Paradox*, 2nd edn. pp. 228–245. Cambridge, MA: Harvard University Press, 1976.

Richardson, Alan. 1941. *The Miracle-Stories of the Gospels*. London: SCM Press.

    1958. *An Introduction to the Theology of the New Testament*. London: SCM Press.

    1966. "The Death of God: A Report Exaggerated." In *Religion in Contemporary Debate*, pp. 102–119. Philadelphia, PA: Westminster Press.

Ridderbos, Herman. 1975. *Paul*, trans. J. R. De Witt. Grand Rapids, MI: Eerdmans.

Robinson, J. Armitage. 1904. *St. Paul's Epistle to the Ephesians*, 2nd edn. London: Macmillan.

Russell, Bertrand. 1903. "A Free Man's Worship." In *Mysticism and Logic*, pp. 44–54. New York: Doubleday, 1957.

    1953. "What Is an Agnostic?" In Louis Greenspan and Stefan Andersson, eds., *Russell on Religion*, pp. 41–49. London: Routledge, 1999.

Sanders, E. P. 1985. *Jesus and Judaism*. Philadelphia, PA: Fortress Press.

    1993. *The Historical Figure of Jesus*. London: Penguin Books.

Savage, Timothy. 1996. *Power through Weakness*. Cambridge University Press.

Schliesser, Benjamin. 2007. *Abraham's Faith in Romans 4*. Tübingen: Mohr Siebeck.

Schweitzer, Albert. 1913. *The Quest of the Historical Jesus*, 2nd edn. trans. John Bowden et al. Minneapolis, MN: Fortress Press, 2001.

Seibert, Eric A. 2009. *Disturbing Divine Behavior: Troubling Old Testament Images of God*. Minneapolis, MN: Fortress Press.

Smith, Ronald Gregor. 1970. *The Doctrine of God*. Philadelphia, PA: Westminster Press.

Spicq, Ceslaus. 1965. *Agapē in the New Testament*, vol. II. London: Herder.

Stern, Jessica. 2003. *Terror in the Name of God*. New York: HarperCollins.

Stewart, James S. 1937. "Hearsay or Experience?" In *Gates of New Life*, pp. 52–63. Edinburgh: T&T Clark.

1940. "Who Is This Jesus? (2)." In *The Strong Name*, pp. 80–89. Edinburgh: T&T Clark.

1969. "Faith and the Strain of Life." In *Walking with God*, ed. Gordon Grant, pp. 209–214. Edinburgh: Saint Andrew Press.

Ward, Ronald A. 1964. *Royal Theology*. London: Marshall, Morgan, & Scott.

Wenham, David. 1995. *Paul: Follower of Jesus or Founder of Christianity?* Grand Rapids, MI: Eerdmans.

2002. *Paul and Jesus*. London: SPCK.

Westerholm, Stephen. 2004. *Perspectives Old and New on Paul*. Grand Rapids, MI: Eerdmans.

Wiebe, Phillip. 2004. *God and Other Spirits*. New York: Oxford University Press.

Williams, Bernard. 1973. "The Makropulos Case: Reflections on the Tedium of Immortality." In *Problems of the Self*, pp. 82–100. Cambridge University Press.

Wittgenstein, Ludwig. 1916. *Notebooks, 1914–1916*, 2nd edn., ed. by G. H. von Wright and G. E. M. Anscombe. University of Chicago Press, 1984.

Index